GLORY DAYS

Black & White

Kevin Lane

Ian Allan PUBLISHING

Front cover:
No L282 (KDD 282E),
a Plaxton-bodied Leyland
Leopard of 1967, pulls out of
Cheltenham Coach Station
on an Associated Motorways
service to Pembroke Dock
on 25 February 1973.
John Jones

Back cover:
Nos 142/1 (DBO 142/1), two
of the Duple Northern-bodied
Leyland Leopards acquired
from Western Welsh in 1971,
pictured at Cheltenham on
25 February 1973 prior to
heading for Bath and
Nottingham respectively.
John Jones

Title page:
All-Leyland TS2 L24
(DF 7555) heads towards
Birmingham *c*1930.
Mike Sutcliffe collection

Contents

First published 2003

ISBN 0 7110 2954 7

All rights reserved. No part of this book may be reproduced or transmitted in any
form or by any means, electronic or mechanical, including photocopying,
recording or by any information storage and retrieval system, without permission
from the Publisher in writing.

© Ian Allan Publishing Ltd 2003

Published by Ian Allan Publishing

an imprint of Ian Allan Publishing Ltd, Hersham, Surrey KT12 4RG.

Printed by Ian Allan Printing Ltd, Hersham, Surrey KT12 4RG.

Code: 0310/B

Introduction

In recent years we have lost many old and familiar names in British coaching; Standerwick, Yelloway of Rochdale, Premier of Cambridge and London's Grey-Green may spring to mind. Perhaps the most stylish operation, due in no small part to the early establishment of a strong overall corporate image, was Cheltenham-based Black & White Motorways — a name that was to survive from the late 1920s through to its virtual abandonment in the 1980s, followed by a brief resurrection and eventual disappearance under Cheltenham & Gloucester. You can't keep a good name down, however, and the name and livery live on in a small way in rural Hampshire. That said, it could be argued that its influence can still be seen on the white National Express coaches operating today.

Incidentally, the use of the term 'Motorways' in the company's title is an interesting one. The first motorway to be opened in Britain was a section of what later became the M6, near Preston. The first section of the M1 was opened in November 1959, with Associated Motorways member BMMO ('Midland Red') beginning its non-stop London Victoria–Birmingham Digbeth motorway service at the same time. However, the term 'Motorways' had been used many years previously by operators to indicate a fast service; Black & White, which, after trading as 'Black & White Luxury Coaches' subsequently dropped this in favour of 'Black & White Motorways', shared this distinction with Mulleys Motorways of Ixworth, Eastern Motorways of Norwich and Pearson's 'Happy Days Motorways' London–Liverpool service, to name but three. That said, a 1939 timetable and guide, in a section entitled 'Associated Motorways and what its organisation means to you', equates the modern motor coach to an old stage coach, following the same old historic highways, and goes on to quote Robert Louis Stevenson's maxim that it is a better thing to travel hopefully than to arrive — perhaps not the image some would find comfortable! Indeed, it is more than a little ironic that it should be the spread of the nation's motorway network that would kill off Cheltenham as an interchange and thus ultimately prove the company's undoing.

Putting this book together has been fascinating, and unravelling the complex nature of operations has not always been easy! In this respect the early years up to the mid-'Thirties and the period from the mid-'Seventies through to Black & White's demise c1990 proved the most difficult; the era of Associated Motorways, with which the history of the company is inextricably linked and under whose auspices all its express services were run from 1934 until 1974 — proved relatively straightforward, but trying to record the events of the turbulent 1980s often threw up more questions than answers! Of course, some would argue that Black & White's 'glory days' were long past by the 1980s, but the later history can be as interesting as the earlier.

Some of the early pictures in this book have, perhaps inevitably, appeared in the past; indeed, I have received the same official views from different sources, having already had them in my own collection! Colour photographs have been difficult to obtain; as one photographer pointed out, one didn't use expensive colour film on a black-and-white coach! Certainly, if there ever was an American tourist on holiday in the Cotswolds in the early 1950s with Kodachrome in his camera who took a picture of the coach in which he travelled, he has eluded me!

Fortunately I have been helped in my researches by a small band of enthusiasts and former Black & White employees who have answered my call for information admirably. Particular thanks are due to Colin Martin and Gerry Serpell-Morris for their help and encouragement and for coming up with some unusual and, in some cases, unique, information and material; also to former Black & White employees Pat Boyle, Tony Neuls and Ian Webber, for their suggestions and reminiscences. All photographs have been credited, but I must mention in particular John Aldridge, John Jones and Mike Greenwood, for allowing me access to their collections.

My usual thanks and appreciation go to Maureen, my wife, for putting up with it all yet again, and to my eldest son Christopher, who was considerate enough to go to university and leave me his room which I now use as an office.

Kevin Lane
Dunstable
July 2003

Cheltenham, the so-called 'centre for the Cotswolds', has a relatively short history. Although granted a market charter in 1226, it was the discovery of a mineral spring in 1716 that resulted in the creation of the spa town. Its reputation was boosted by the visit of King George III in 1788, while the Duke of Wellington was another to recommend the medicinal properties of its waters. Thus was born the finest Regency town in England. However, for those of us with an interest in the history of road transport, Cheltenham is synonymous with coach operator Black & White Motorways and its coach station, hub of the Associated Motorways network.

The man behind Black & White Motorways was one George Readings. Born in 1893, he joined the Forces in 1914 in the Army Service Corps. After the war he returned to his Surrey home and by 1920 was running an ex-War Department Model T Ford, converted to carry eight passengers, the three miles between Ewhurst and Cranleigh. Business increased, and the route later ran from Cranleigh to Guildford and competed with Aldershot & District route 23, which also ran between the two towns but by a different route. Trading originally as 'Readings' Garage' and later as 'Royal Blue', Readings eventually settled on 'Surrey Hills Motor Services'. Further expansion in the area included services also serving Dorking and Horsham and saw the arrival of five new Lancia buses. However, the new network was seriously treading on the collective toes of Aldershot & District and East Surrey, the latter as a subsidiary of the London General Omnibus Co. A buyout was, perhaps, inevitable, and, in a complex agreement, Aldershot & District acquired the routes, the garage in Ewhurst and the five Lancias (two of which subsequently passed to the LGOC) in January 1926.

George Readings and his wife subsequently travelled to Ireland to investigate the need for a bus service between Belfast and the border with Eire. As it happened, the service had already been started by another operator, but the visit was by no means a waste of time. Readings had been impressed by the sight of an all-white coach and had hit on the idea of adding a touch of black to the livery to create a distinctive image.

Back in England, the Readings moved to Cheltenham, and George put his ideas into practice. He opened a garage in nearby Charlton Kings and a booking office at 411 High Street, Cheltenham, and began local tours and excursions under the name 'Black & White Luxury Coaches'. The vehicle chosen to begin operations — a Reo Sprinter 14-seater — had also been influenced by the trip to Ireland, where he had noted a number of small American buses in service with independent operators. Interestingly, this first Reo carried a Surrey registration, suggesting Readings did not immediately sever all ties with his former home. Later in 1926 two further Reos — this time with 21-seat London Lorries bodywork — were added and began a service to London in November that year.

Long-distance coach travel was not a new phenomenon, and by the early 1920s a number of regular services were operating, almost all radiating from London. Although there were few restrictions other than regulations set by local police forces, the maximum speed limit for coaches (as set by the Heavy Motor Car Order of 1904) was just 12mph. In October 1928 this was increased to 20mph, but only for vehicles running on pneumatic tyres. (This inevitably led to the swift disappearance from the streets of solid-rubber-tyred coaches, for which the limit remained 12mph; solid-metal-tyred vehicles were restricted to a mere 8mph.) The 1930 Road Traffic Act would increase the maximum limit still further, to 30mph.

One service investigated by George Readings was that operated by Greyhound Motors Ltd between Bristol (and later Weston-

super-Mare) and London, terminating at the Clarendon Hotel in Hammersmith Broadway. This had begun in February 1925, and both company and service were to be acquired by Bristol Tramways & Carriage Co Ltd in March 1928, initially remaining as a separate company. As we shall see, Bristol became part owner of Black & White in 1930.

For his London service, Readings offered an 8.45pm departure from Cheltenham (Cambray) via Burford, Witney, Oxford, Henley, Maidenhead and Slough, with a return to Cheltenham from Hammersmith Broadway (at the Greyhound Motors booking office) at 2pm. (The early return was apparently to enable Oxford to be reached before dark, as passengers did not like travelling at night.) The service ran six days a week and took around 4 hours at a fare of 8s 6d single and 14s return — 42½p and 70p respectively in today's money. The Great Western Railway service to London Paddington, running via Gloucester and Swindon, took, at best, around 3 hours, with a single fare of 14s 3d.

It should perhaps be mentioned here that there was another service from London to Gloucester via Oxford and Cheltenham, operated by Rural England Motor Coaches Ltd of Ealing. This appears to have commenced in the spring of 1927. A timetable from 10 July 1927 offers one return journey each day, leaving Gloucester at 10am and arriving at London (Shepherd's Bush) at 3.30pm; the return journey left London at 2pm, reaching Gloucester at 7.30pm. From a distance the company crest looked suspiciously like that used by Black & White, being circular, with fleetname within, and 'wings'. The service ceased early in 1930, probably taken over by Great Western Express, itself bought out by Red & White in 1932.

On 12 April 1928 George Readings registered Black & White Motorways Ltd, with its registered address at Paris House, The Promenade, Cheltenham. From the outset, a very positive image was developed which was to become a classic in the coaching industry. The basic livery was, of course, black and white, applied in a simple but distinctive style. The fleetname ('Luxury Coaches' having been dropped) included of a winged shield, derived from the Reo badge, with 'BW' intertwined in white on black within. Above this was 'BLACK & WHITE' and 'MOTORWAYS Ltd' below. The shield was applied to the sides and rear of the vehicle, whilst another appeared above the front destination screen. This image was extended to other aspects, particularly to advertising and property, including, ultimately, the frontage of the coach station at Cheltenham.

Before long, two return journeys (later increased to three) were operating between Cheltenham and London and included a Sunday service. From the summer of 1927 luxury coach tours were also operating to Bournemouth and Weston-super-Mare, while towards the end of the year the Black & White head office and departure point in Cheltenham had moved to Paris House. From the end of 1927 and throughout 1928 there was a veritable explosion of new routes. December 1927 saw a daily service from Great Malvern and Tewkesbury to London, extended the following February to Worcester. Gloucester, Ross-on-Wye and Hereford were also added, as was Weston-super-Mare in June 1928. The cramped facilities at the London end were abandoned in favour of a new terminus at nearby Hammersmith Bridge Road in July 1928. The roll-call of new destinations continued — Ludlow, Leominster and Bromyard; Leicester via Stratford and Warwick; Nuneaton and Hinckley; Leamington via Kenilworth and Coventry; Birmingham via Droitwich; Cardiff from Gloucester via Lydney, Chepstow and Newport. By 1929 Bournemouth, Northampton, Shrewsbury, Wolverhampton, Derby and Nottingham had been added, all with connections arranged at Cheltenham. In order to compete with the railways, coaches delivered in 1929/30 were finished to a de luxe specification, including toilet facilities and even a chocolate-vending machine. Copies of such newspapers as *The Tatler* and *The Illustrated London News* were also provided by the company on these services, being unsold stock supplied free by the publisher.

With the tentacles of the Black & White empire reaching further and further afield, a good network of booking agents was essential, and this was developed from 1929. An early arrangement with the bookshop chain W. H. Smith & Son proved successful, although existing travel agents tended to be less keen, due to their allegiance to the railway companies. A list of booking agents on a 1930 leaflet included a number of post offices and such businesses as Shakespear's Gramophone Shop in Gloucester, F. W. Watts & Sons, Confectioners, Hereford, and The Lawton Cycle & Motor Co, 195 High Street, Brentford, Middlesex.

The rapid expansion of the company brought its own problems in that there simply wasn't enough capital to put future plans into

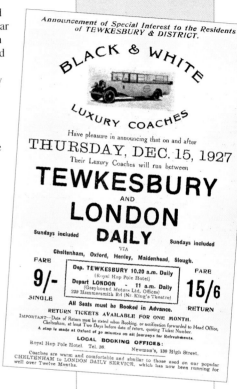

The new order with a vengeance! A trio of Leyland Tiger TS2 coaches, led by all-Leyland L32 (DF 8186) of 1929, appear in what is possibly a publicity photograph. They are presumably stationary and the Rolls-Royce is slowly overtaking; what price for any of them in preservation today?
Mike Sutcliffe collection

practice. This led George Readings to sell his interests in Black & White Motorways to the Birmingham & Midland Motor Omnibus Co Ltd and move on to pastures new. Unable to operate similar services in England or Wales due to a restrictive covenant included in the contract, he initially set up another company, Blue & White Coaches Ltd, operating tours and private hires from premises in Chiswick High Road, London W4. In this venture he was assisted by Arthur E. King, the former Black & White manager in London. The enterprise was apparently not a success, despite the experience of the two men, and Readings later bought and developed the Regent Motors garage business in Cheltenham. He subsequently joined the town council, being elected an alderman in 1955 and Mayor in 1956. Retiring from public life in 1967, he remained in Cheltenham, where he died in April 1981, aged 87.

The vehicles

The first vehicle bought in 1926 was the little Reo Sprinter used initially on tours around Cheltenham. It was registered in Surrey as PF 2244 and was later converted into a box van. Two further Reos soon followed, numbered 1 and 2 (later R1/2) and were registered DF 248/9. They were 21-seaters bodied by London Lorries and saw use on the new London service, lasting in the fleet until 1932. These were so-called 'all weather' coaches, the canvas roof being pulled back on warm days, although how often this was actually done is not recorded. Passengers were, however, all supplied with a rug! Service expansion saw eight new vehicles enter the fleet; these comprised four Reos, numbered 3, 4, 7 and 9 (later R3/4/7/9) and registered DF 2290/1, 2955, 3127, a couple of Gilfords as 5 and 8 (later G5/8), registered DF 2667, 3059, and two 'one-offs' — 6 (later S6), a Studebaker, registered DF 2892, and 10, a Graham Dodge, registered DF 3285. All were bodied by London Lorries with the exception of the Studebaker, which carried Strachan & Brown

ALL-WEATHER COACHES.
Accommodating from 14 to 32 passengers, supplied on seasonal terms.

bodywork. The following year saw deliveries split between Reo — R10-5 (DF 4837, 5165/85/6, 5335/6) — and Gilford — G16-21 (DF 5337/8, 5559, 5734-6). No R13 carried a Weymann body, otherwise London Lorries was again favoured.

Black & White's last year as an independent company saw the delivery of Bence-bodied Star VB4 Flyer No S40 (DF 8747); by this time, Star was owned by Guy Motors. However, the principal deliveries of 1929 were no fewer than 18 Leyland-bodied Leyland Tiger TS2 coaches, which set a new standard. Numbered L22-39, they were registered DF 7051, 7244, 7555-7, 7840/1, 8013-5, 8186, 8300/91, 8418-22. Their Leyland bodywork was fitted out by specialist contractor Abbotts of Farnham (in George Readings' old Surrey stamping-ground), and the interiors were very well appointed, with such details as flower vases, curtains, chocolate-vending machines and the provision of newspapers and magazines all giving the impression of a quality product. Black & White was competing principally with the railways, so facilities and the level of comfort had to be comparable. Seats were initially covered in moquette, but this was found to be less hygienic and more difficult to clean than leather, the material subsequently used — after all, if it was good enough for the cars of the day, it was good enough for those travelling on coaches. Notable (if not unique) among coach operation of the period was the provision of toilets. Such facilities were deemed essential by the company, particularly when children were on board. The less desirable option was frequent stops built into the timetable, something the competing railway service did not have to do. It was also found by the company that the toilet gave passengers somewhere to go if they needed to stretch their legs.

DF 3285, the solitary Graham-Dodge with 14-seat London Lorries body, bought new in 1927 and pictured from a contemporary advertisement. It lasted five years with Black & White before passing to Bunty, Coventry, in 1932.
Ian Webber collection

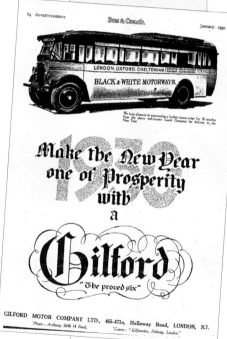

64 ADVERTISEMENTS

Bus & Coach

January, 1930

LONDON. OXFORD. CHELTENHAM
BLACK & WHITE MOTORWAYS.

We have pleasure in announcing a further repeat order for 10 coaches from the above well-known Coach Company for delivery in the New Year.

Make the New Year one of Prosperity with a Gilford

1930

"The proved six"

GILFORD MOTOR COMPANY LTD., 465-471a, Holloway Road, LONDON, N.7.
'Phone : Archway 2646 (4 lines). 'Grams : "Gilfomotor, Holway, London."

7

A splendid early view at Cheltenham, with a pair of all-Leyland Tiger TS2s loading for Torquay and London. Amid the fascinating 1920s fashion parade is another gem: S40 (DF 8747), the Bence-bodied Star VB4, is just visible on the right, probably on excursion or tour duty.
John Aldridge collection

Another Cheltenham view, taken at the same time as the previous picture. All-Leyland TS2 No L29 (DF 8013) is on its way to Swansea, while on the right is 1930 Gilford/London Lorries G46 (DG 407). The Star is behind the Gilford.
John Aldridge collection

2. From Associated Motorways to National Bus Company

On 30 April 1930 Black & White Motorways was sold for the sum of £100,000 to the Birmingham & Midland Motor Omnibus Co Ltd (BMMO), which then sold 40% of the company to the Bristol Tramways & Carriage Co Ltd and 20% to City of Oxford Motor Services. However, such was the quality of the Black & White image that there was no intention of dividing the company between its new owners, and the company would remain a separate entity for nearly half a century.

The first major development under the new management was the opening of Cheltenham Coach Station, in June 1931. Dedicated coach stations were uncommon at this time, and those that did exist tended to be in the cities. However, efforts to find an alternative terminus in Cheltenham had begun as early as 1929, as Paris House was already being found inadequate. St Margaret's, a Georgian mansion house in St Margaret's Road, was actually purchased in 1930 by George Readings, along with

some 3½ acres of land. Conveniently located in the town centre, it was accessible both from St Margaret's Road and from North Place — a useful feature, as traffic congestion was a consideration even then.

The house itself was extensively rebuilt for its new role. The ground floor included the booking office, waiting room, a buffet and toilet facilities. On the first floor were a café, a lounge and the kitchens, while the company offices were located on the top floor. A 'house style' featuring black and white decoration was used throughout, even down to specially designed furniture and staff uniforms.

The exterior was painted white and also featured black and white detailing, the Black & White winged shield being prominent above the entrance porch. Such a building would be given listed status today and reconstruction would not have been permitted, but by all accounts it was a striking addition to facilities in the town.

The coach station in 1930, with a pair of new Leyland Tigers loading, including L36 (DF 8419) preparing to leave for Torquay. How unhurried it all looks when compared with the postwar scene!
John Aldridge collection

The grounds, which had previously included a tennis court and stables, were largely concreted over and allowed ample space for coaches to assemble and load. At the opposite corner of the site to the mansion was built a garage (the so-called 'brewery garage') where everything including heavy overhauls could be undertaken and a paintshop was later established; the garage would also be used as a departure point for Yelloway services on summer Saturdays. The building incorporated the traffic office, allowing a fine view over the station In addition, there was room for visiting coaches and private cars at a daily rate of one shilling (5p) and sixpence (2½p) respectively.

In 1932/3 Black & White acquired three operators, thus further consolidating its position. The first of these, early in 1932, was Ensign Motor Coaches, London W10, which brought a daily service between London and Aberystwyth (described in contemporary promotional literature as variously the 'Biarritz of Wales' and the 'Athens of Wales' — perhaps a little over the top!). Taking nearly 12 hours (as against just over seven by rail), the journey was via Chipping Norton, Moreton-in-Marsh, Broadway, Evesham, Worcester, Bromyard, Leominster and Llandrindod Wells; this was the first Black & White service not to call at Cheltenham. In 1933 Black & White purchased Link Safety Coaches of Bournemouth, bringing a Birmingham–

Bournemouth service, while later the same year came the joint acquisition, with Red & White Services, of South Wales Express Coaches of London W12, whose service between London and Llanelli via Oxford, Cheltenham, Gloucester and Cardiff ran in direct competition.

As was touched upon in the previous chapter, by the late 1920s long-distance coach services had become a viable alternative to

▲ Another prewar view at Cheltenham, with Bristol JO6G/Burlingham B81 (BAD 635) seen shortly after arrival. Passengers disperse with their luggage, one or two disappearing into the café on the right. *Author's collection*

▲ Cheltenham in 1934, from the opposite direction to that in the previous picture, with the café on the left and refuelling bays and inspection pits to the right. *John Aldridge collection*

◄ A closer view of the café; the complete Black & White image is evident here, with the chequered tiling and general decoration. Even the seats are the correct colours! A few menus can just be read on the windows: a 'special lunch' is 1s 6d (7p), while for 8d (around 3p) one could have had poached egg on toast with a cup of tea or coffee. *John Aldridge collection*

▲ An attractive line-up of cars and a van under the canopy at Cheltenham in October 1932. The three cars on the left are M1-3 (DG 4716-8), 1932 Morris Minors, whilst the two on the right are A4/A5 (PD 3265, RK 9401), Austin 20s which came with Ensign. The van (RX 7765) was acquired with South Wales Express. The Morris cars were used by inspectors, but the Austins were licensed as PSVs and saw use on feeder services. The two Austins were sold in 1936 for £40, but the trio of Morris cars fetched rather more — £114 — a year later. Details visible behind the vehicles include a cigarette machine (6d and 1s) and a machine which will tell your fortune ('you are going on a long journey?') and weight, while directly above is the Verandah Café. *John Aldridge collection*

the railways. Not only was it possible to travel to all corners of the country (even at the height of the railways' supremacy, not everywhere was accessible by train); coach tours to the Continent had been operating since the end of World War 1. As the 1920s progressed, bus and coach services were becoming something of a free-for-all, and the introduction of new legislation was required to limit wasteful competition. An operator wishing to run a service between two towns was at the mercy of the various local authorities *en route*, which were empowered to inspect (and hopefully pass) each vehicle to travel through their area. The 1930 Road Traffic Act required each operator to obtain a licence for each route and to justify itself to the newly appointed Traffic Commissioners, organised into 13 Traffic Areas. Under the new system, the Commissioners would grant a licence only after the submission of route details, fares to be charged and so on; objections would be heard from interested parties, including the police, other operators and the railways, and all the information weighed up before a decision was made. In some cases, operators of established services would find themselves unable to obtain licences; indeed, more than one operator would often apply to work on the same route. Initially, there was a lot of rationalisation and consolidation, many small operators ceasing to trade or selling up, but eventually the situation settled down. The legal maximum speed limit for coaches, increased from 12mph to 20mph in 1928, was increased again to 30mph from the beginning of 1931.

In some areas there was still room for further co-ordination of services, not least to combat a vigorous advertising campaign then being undertaken by the railways. In 1932 Black & White entered into preliminary talks with Red & White Services of Chepstow concerning routes between London and South Wales;

Black & White ran from Cheltenham to Cardiff and Swansea, while Red & White operated a number of services into South Wales from Gloucester. Prior to this, Black & White had inaugurated a scheme whereby passengers from the London–Cheltenham service could make through bookings into South and West Wales using various stage-carriage operators, including Western Welsh, Eastern Valleys and South Wales Transport. Further discussions took place over the following two years between various operators running express services from the Midlands, the North West and London to the South West and South Wales.

The outcome was the formation on 1 July 1934 of Associated Motorways, whereby six operators agreed to pool certain services. The original members were Black & White Motorways, Red & White Services, Elliott Bros (Royal Blue), Greyhound Motor Services, Birmingham & Midland Motor Omnibus Co (BMMO — 'Midland Red') and United Counties Omnibus Co. On 1 January 1935 the Elliott brothers sold out to Thomas Tilling, the express routes passing to Western National and

Black & White Motorways map *c*1934.
John Aldridge collection

13

BLACK & WHITE
MIDLAND "RED"
RED & WHITE
AND
GREYHOUND
JOINT SERVICES

REGULAR DAILY SERVICES FROM

DERBY, BURTON-ON-TRENT, LICHFIELD,
WOLVERHAMPTON, BIRMINGHAM,
BROMSGROVE, DROITWICH, WORCESTER,
MALVERN, UPTON-ON-SEVERN, TEWKESBURY

TO ALL PARTS OF THE

SOUTH COAST

OFFICIAL AGENTS:—

MARCH 19th, until APRIL 30th, 1934.

Joint Services leaflet
1934.
*Gerry Serpell-Morris
collection*

Southern National (the excursion licences passing to Hants & Dorset), the number of Associated Motorways participants being thus increased to seven. (Two further members — Lincolnshire Road Car and Eastern Counties, with routes to Cheltenham from Scunthorpe and Cambridge respectively — would join in 1956.) Each constituent was allotted a percentage of mileage to be run and revenue received — Black & White's share being the greatest, at just under 40% in both cases — calculated on 1933 figures.

Black & White placed all of its express services under Associated Motorways control, these being:

London to Aberystwyth via Worcester
(not serving Cheltenham)
Cheltenham–Hereford–Aberystwyth
Cheltenham–Newport–Cardiff–Swansea
Cheltenham–Oxford–London
Cheltenham–Stroud–Bath–Bournemouth
Cheltenham–Swindon–Salisbury–Southampton–
Portsmouth–Southsea
Cheltenham–Bath–Exeter–Torquay–Paignton
Cheltenham–Bristol–Weston-super-Mare
Cheltenham–Hereford–Ludlow–Shrewsbury
Cheltenham–Worcester–Derby
Cheltenham–Birmingham–Wolverhampton
Cheltenham–Coventry–Leicester–Nottingham
Cheltenham–Banbury–Northampton–Kettering

Also included was a day excursion from Cheltenham to Weston-super-Mare.

The hub of the network was Cheltenham, ideally located (being roughly equidistant from Lancashire and the West Country and from London and South Wales) and with an almost new, covered coach station. In 1933 it dealt with around 350,000 passengers, the expectation being that the annual figure would rise within a couple of years to between 2 and 3 million. Associated Motorways' management was accommodated in offices at the coach station, alongside Black & White's.

The co-ordination of services gave passengers access to hundreds of destinations, with just one change of coach, at Cheltenham, where services were dovetailed to connect with other services at key times during the day. (These would vary

over the years; in the early 1950s, for example, departures were at 10.45am, 2.00pm, 4.30pm and 7pm, with a few different night departures also.) Through ticketing was essential, of course; as far as licensing was concerned, it was agreed after much discussion with the various Area Traffic Commissioners that each route would be granted a single licence, issued in the name of 'the companies comprising Associated Motorways', with all the joint operators listed on the licence. (This arrangement — unusual, if not unique, as the Traffic Commissioners normally insisted on the issue of separate licences to joint operators — would last until the abolition of Associated Motorways in 1974.) The co-ordination extended to timetables and inter-availability of tickets. An overall image was developed, taking a lead, perhaps, from Black & White (certainly in the use of the term 'Motorways'), while publicity was branded in a unified style of green, orange and black — not as bad as it sounds! — the colours being chosen to avoid appearing to favour any one member of the group. However, early publicity, albeit under the collective headline of 'Associated Motorways', differentiated between members. Thus leaflet BW34 advertised the service from London to South Wales and the West Country as operated by Black & White and Red & White, in association with the other four members. All constituents retained their separate identities rather than adopt a new, overall image.

Booking was through the offices of the constituent companies and of other operators not part of the pool, such as Hants & Dorset and Southdown, as well as through travel agents, such as Thomas Cook, and other agents, shops and post offices, of which Black & White had developed a good network in the early days. It was quite a job to keep all these agents up-to-date with publicity material, and agency bulletins would be issued to advise of special instructions. An unusual opportunity for publicity (at least for the time) presented itself in 1938, when a team from the BBC visited Cheltenham to record an outside broadcast of operations at the coach station on Whit Monday. The 4.30pm departures were chosen and all aspects were covered, including the café, the maintenance bays and the drivers' canteen, where there was a discussion on the merits of oil *vs* petrol engines! Has this recording survived, I wonder?

H. R. Lapper, Director and General Manager of Black & White Motorways and, later, Chairman of the Committee of Management of Associated Motorways (until 1952) had interesting views on the whole set-up. Writing in *Coaching Journal* in 1973, he expressed regret at some of the arrangements. He would have preferred that the organisation be operated by Black & White in order to present the public with an overall image already well established, rather than use green, orange and black for publicity, with each member of the pool operating in its own livery. As Black & White had no express services of its own outside the pool, some of its regular passengers would, he felt, not be aware from publicity that they would still be able to travel in the company's coaches. Furthermore, the disciplines of Black & White operating staff could not be imposed on those of the other members. Strict regulations concerning (for example) smoking on duty and the wearing of full uniform would sometimes be at odds with what would be tolerated from drivers operating other Associated services. Between 1930 and 1934 coach attendants were employed and were responsible for such duties as passenger supervision, ticket issue, keeping the coach clean and tidy, emptying the toilet and so on, travelling with the vehicle and carrying on these tasks when terminating away from Cheltenham; this practice was reluctantly abolished to conform to the normal standards of the Associated operators. However,

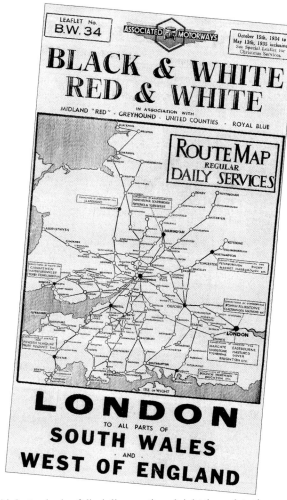

high standards of discipline continued right through to the National Travel era; woe betide the driver who turned up to work in anything other than his full uniform. Even if his shift pattern had kept him away from home for days, he was expected to keep up standards: if he hadn't got a clean white shirt to wear then he went and bought one! The meticulous Black & White image even extended to cap badges, tie-pins and cufflinks.

From September 1939, with the onset of war, operations were gradually reduced, fuel rationing and a reduction in services

It's 1946, and the transport industry is starting on the long road to recovery after the war. On Thursday 12 September Bristol L6G/ECW B97 (CDG 374) has arrived at Cheltenham and is laying over before its next duty.
Bryan C. Boyle

Associated Motorways timetable 1939.
Gerry Serpell-Morris collection

being the order of the day, and the first casualties were night services, tours and excursions. Associated Motorways became concerned more with cross-country routes, and in 1940 Black & White assumed responsibility for all the services and duplicate mileage operated by Midland Red. However, petrol rationing for private motoring led to an increase in coach travel, and, despite the restrictions in force, the revenue received in 1941 was the highest since 1934. From October 1942, however, all services were suspended, such was the national need to conserve fuel and rubber. For the rest of the war, those Black & White vehicles still running were involved mainly in troop movements etc, while five of the 1929 Leyland Tiger TS2s had already (in August 1939) been converted to ambulances (painted grey and with seats replaced by racks to carry stretchers), in readiness for the expected immediate aerial bombardment.

As far as Cheltenham was concerned, the bombardment came on the night of 11 December 1940, when high-explosives fell on the town and completely destroyed the old mansion-house part of the coach station — despite camouflage, the site no doubt presented a distinctive target. Bristol JO6G No B79 was badly damaged in the attack but was later rebodied. Another Bristol had been caught in an air-raid on London on 7 September 1940 and had all of its windows blown out, despite which it was driven back to Cheltenham, neither the driver nor his sole passenger being hurt.

For the second half of the war both the Black & White fleet and coach station were under-utilised (part of the site being used for the construction of nose sections for Bristol aircraft), although plans for a resumption of services were underway from mid-1944 following the Allied invasion of Europe.

The postwar resumption of Associated Motorways Services took place from 3 June 1946, offering a modest service of one return journey per day (in most cases) on 26 routes; half of these services were timed to arrive at Cheltenham at between 1.15 and 1.30pm, to allow a 2pm interchange. Night services to South Wales were reintroduced from 14 October.

Petrol rationing for private motoring remained in force until 1950, so for a brief few years the motor coach (and the railways) could fulfil the needs of the travelling public. Such was the shortage of vehicles, however, that seats had to be booked at least seven days in advance and that open-date return tickets would not be issued.

A view across the coach station at Cheltenham in 1951, from the offices of H. R. Lapper, then General Manager of Black & White and Chairman of the Associated Motorways Management Committee. The time is 1.40pm and coaches are in position for the 2 o'clock departure. Black & White vehicles are well to the fore, with contributions from Midland Red and Bristol Tramways. All visible vehicles appear to be postwar, judging by the lack of roof-mounted luggage racks. *John Aldridge collection*

At five minutes past two, all is calm again. A United Counties Bristol LWL disappears off to the left, whilst on the extreme right is a Red & White Albion. A good view is afforded of the station, the prominent gap being where the house once stood. A temporary booking office has been built under the canopy, and there is a large departure board on the wall outside the ladies' toilets. *John Aldridge collection*

TIME TABLE

DAY AND NIGHT SERVICES
LONDON
TO ALL PARTS OF
SOUTH WALES
and **WEST OF ENGLAND**

DAILY SERVICES
MIDLANDS
TO ALL PARTS OF
SOUTH COAST
and **SOUTH WALES**

ASSOCIATED MOTORWAYS
BLACK & WHITE · RED & WHITE · MIDLAND RED
ROYAL BLUE · BRISTOL TRAMWAYS · UNITED COUNTIES

OFFICIAL BOOKING & ENQUIRY AGENTS

1947
WINTER SERVICES
October 13th–December 31st

▲ Associated Motorways timetable 1947.
Gerry Serpell-Morris collection

▶ Associated Motorways timetable leaflet 1951/2 (Midlands/South Coast).
John Aldridge collection

WINTER SERVICES—8th Oct., 1951 to 25th May, 1952

BLACK & WHITE
RED & WHITE
MIDLAND RED

ASSOCIATED MOTORWAYS

UNITED COUNTIES
ROYAL BLUE
BRISTOL TRAMWAYS

Regular Daily Services
(SUNDAYS INCLUDED)
from
CHELTENHAM
TO ALL PARTS OF
MIDLANDS and SOUTH COAST

(detailed route timetables — Cheltenham–Banbury–Northampton–Kettering; Cheltenham–Coventry–Leicester–Nottingham; Cheltenham–Worcester–Birmingham–Walsall–Derby; Cheltenham–Malvern–Dudley–Wolverhampton–Stafford; Cheltenham–Weston–Taunton–Exeter–Paignton; Cheltenham–Bath–Warminster–Poole–Bournemouth; Cheltenham–Devizes–Salisbury–Bournemouth; Cheltenham–Salisbury–Southampton–Portsmouth)

Royal Blue Connection—A departs 30 minutes earlier. B departs 10 minutes earlier. C Departs 26 minutes Later. } For period 8th to 21st October and 1st to 25th May.

FOR SERVICES TO LONDON AND ALL PARTS SOUTH WALES—see over

Full particulars of all Associated Motorways Routes, Fares, etc on application to—
RED & WHITE SERVICES LTD., NORTH STREET. Tel. 3047.
BRISTOL TRAMWAYS & CARRIAGE CO. LTD., CLARENCE STREET. Tel. 2021.

WINTER, 1950-51 SERVICES   CURRENT 1st OCTOBER — 14th JANUARY.

ASSOCIATED MOTORWAYS
BLACK & WHITE · RED & WHITE · MIDLAND RED
ROYAL BLUE · BRISTOL TRAMWAYS · UNITED COUNTIES

REGULAR DAY & NIGHT SERVICES
DEPARTING FROM LONDON COASTAL COACHES LTD.
VICTORIA COACH STATION
BUCKINGHAM PALACE ROAD, S.W.1.

LONDON
TO

ABERDARE	CIRENCESTER	KINGTON	PENYGRAIG
ABERGAVENNY	COWBRIDGE	LEOMINSTER	PONTYPOOL
ABERCYNON	CAERWENT	LLANDRINDOD WELLS	PONTYPRIDD
BLACKWOOD	CRUMLIN	LECHLADE	PORTH
BLAKENEY	DOWLAIS	LYDNEY	PORT TALBOT
BRIDGEND	DINAS	MALVERN	ROSS-ON-WYE
BRITON FERRY	EBBW VALE	MERTHYR	STROUD
BRYNMAWR	EVESHAM	MORRISTON	SWANSEA
BURFORD	GILWERN	NEATH	TONYPANDY
CARDIFF	GLOUCESTER	NELSON	TREDEGAR
CHELTENHAM	GLYNNEATH	NEWBRIDGE	TREHERBERT
CHEPSTOW	HIRWAUN	NEWPORT	UPTON-ON-SEVERN
COLEFORD	HEREFORD	OXFORD	USK
CINDERFORD	HANLEY CASTLE	PENTRE	WORCESTER

For complete Routes and Destinations served, Times, Fares, Etc., see over
LOCAL AGENT.

Head Office: ASSOCIATED MOTORWAYS, CHELTENHAM Tel. 3067

▲ Associated Motorways timetable leaflet 1950/1 (London).
John Aldridge collection

CAFE FACILITIES

ARE AVAILABLE **DAILY**
INCLUDING SUNDAYS

*PRIVATE PARTIES ESPECIALLY CATERED FOR
AT ALL TIMES — BY ARRANGEMENT*

For full information apply to:—
BLACK & WHITE MOTORWAYS, LTD.
COACH STATION
ST. MARGARET'S ROAD, CHELTENHAM SPA
Telephone: Cheltenham 3067

▲ Associated Motorways
timetable 1954.
Gerry Serpell-Morris collection

▲ Associated Motorways
Luxury Travel advert.
Author's collection

Bristol JO6G/Burlingham B85 (BAD 638) runs over Corporation tram tracks on the run into Birmingham in 1951. *D. F. Parker*

Journey's end in Birmingham was the Midland Red coach station at Digbeth. With PMT and Midland Red double-deckers for company, 1937 Bristol JO6G/Burlingham B87 (CDD 2) lays over in 1953. *D. F. Parker*

▲ As recounted earlier, the old St Margaret's House part of the coach station was destroyed by enemy action in 1940. After the war a temporary booking office was erected which remained in use until replaced by a new office block erected on the site of the old house and opened in January 1956, incorporating a booking hall, waiting room, and left-luggage office. The café at the back ▼ of the house was also thoroughly refurbished; this had escaped the bombing and had reopened when services resumed in 1946.

It was the practice for routes to be reallocated each winter and summer season between the Associated Motorways pool members, adjustments being made to keep mileage figures at the correct levels; the service from Cheltenham to Pembroke Dock, for example, was the responsibility of Black & White in the winter

but of Red & White in the summer. Black & White did, however, operate a number of regular routes, including those from Cheltenham to Derby, Nottingham/Mansfield, Bournemouth and Portsmouth, as well as most London journeys, although night runs were worked jointly with Red & White. Although Black & White vehicles could be found regularly on these services, they could turn up as duplicates on almost any route; when pool members had run out of vehicles, or when large numbers of duplicates were required, hirings would be undertaken from local independent operators. The coach, with driver, would be hired to Black & White, which in turn would claim the cost of the hiring back from Associated Motorways. Operators involved in such hirings over the years included Perrett of Shipton Oliffe; Cottrells of Mitcheldean; Edwards of Joy's Green; Warner's of Tewkesbury; Barry's of Moreton-in-Marsh; Say of Gloucester and Pulham's of Bourton-on-the-Water.

In addition to its work for Associated Motorways, Black & White was very active in the field of tours and excursions, which was how it had started out. Cheltenham was (and still is) a tourist attraction in its own right, and the tours were aimed at both visitors and residents. For some years, these were operated in association with Bristol (Greyhound), which later withdrew from the agreement. Comprehensive booklets were published each year, giving details of itineraries from both Cheltenham and Gloucester. The bulk of this work consisted of half- and full-day tours, which ran from the beginning of April through to the end of October. Many of these tours would be of the Cotswolds, of which up to 10 different itineraries would be advertised. Other destinations included Bristol Zoo, Coventry Cathedral, Blenheim Palace, Stratford-upon-Avon and Hereford, while the Forest of Dean was especially promoted during the autumn. Various excursions were also operated, to end up rather further afield; thus Black & White vehicles could be seen in such diverse locations as Swanage, The Mumbles, Barry Island, London Airport, Aberystwyth and Whipsnade Zoo. An eight-day luxury tour was also offered to North Wales and Snowdonia. In the winter a few vehicles would be occupied on trips to the pantomimes and theatres.

Private hire was another important activity for Black & White, and a comprehensive booklet was published, suggesting a wide variety of attractions. Most private hires were, of course, geared to specific events. The Cheltenham Gold Cup race meeting for instance, held over three days each March, generated a tremendous amount of work for local operators (and, indeed, still does). Black & White had a contract with Tully's Travel

Leyland Royal Tiger L129 (KDF 980) seen in June 1954 on arrival at Swansea on the daily service from London. This run was something of a marathon, leaving Victoria at 10.15am and not reaching Swansea (United Welsh bus station) until 8.00pm. The return service to London would leave the next morning at 9.45am to arrive at 7.30pm. This particular service was one that did not call at Cheltenham, running non-stop between High Wycombe and Caerwent.
D. F. Parker

Although Black & White regularly hired vehicles in, it did sometimes loan them out. In February and March 1963, for instance, seven of the 1957 Willowbrook-bodied AEC Reliances were loaned to City of Oxford Motor Services, the severe winter having caused a vehicle shortage (other vehicles being loaned by South Midland and Smiths of Reading). A196 (SDF 196), bearing a prominent 'ON HIRE' label, waits at Oxford Gloucester Green.
Mike Greenwood collection

Summer Saturdays would usually involve substantial hirings to Associated Motorways from local independent operators. One such was Cottrell's Coaches, Mitcheldean, owner of PAD 267, a Burlingham-bodied AEC Reliance, seen at Cheltenham on 24 August 1963.
Mike Sutcliffe

Agency of Carlow, Co Wicklow, to transport 'punters' from Birmingham Airport to their hotels and to and from the racecourse each day. This required around a dozen coaches, and it was probably quite a job getting everyone home again in the evening! It was not unknown for particular drivers to be requested for such jobs; no doubt they were much sought-after for their local betting knowledge . . . !

From 1927 the booking office and departure point for the tours was at Paris House, The Promenade. The office continued in use after the opening of the coach station in 1931 and did not close until May 1980, when bookings were transferred to the coach station. (Of note was the 21in-long model of Bristol L6G/Duple JDD 490 that once stood in the window at Paris House; made of moulded compressed-laminate paper, it was the work of Edgley Studios, Cheltenham, and survives today in private ownership.) The best — usually the newest — vehicles were used for tour work, which required the hiring of vehicles from other operators to fulfil Associated Motorways commitments. A pool of drivers employed on tour work was established, based on seniority — a highly prized position. A driver might be allocated a particular coach for a season and, as well as driving, would undertake other duties such as providing a running commentary.

B94 (CDG 371), first of the 1938 Bristol L6G/ECW coaches, pictured on tour duty at Winchcombe in 1950. The lady boarding happens to be Mrs Lapper, sister-in-law of General Manager H. R. Lapper, although this was not an official view. *Colin Martin collection*

Black & White's booking office in The Promenade, Cheltenham, seen in NBC days in 1975. *Mike Greenwood*

Coach to Pantos leaflet and Black & White Private Hire Handbook *Colln Martin collection*

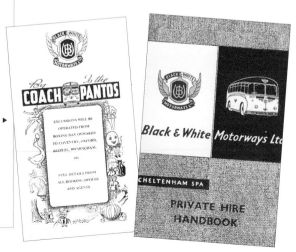

Luxury Coach Tours

from Cheltenham & Gloucester 1965

▲ Luxury Coach Tours booklet 1965. *Colin Martin collection*

◄ Private hire was an important feature of Black & White's operations, with a regularly published handbook provided to suggest itineraries. AEC Reliance/Willowbrook A195 (SDF 195) poses in the pretty half-timbered Worcestershire village of Elmley Castle, near Evesham, in 1957. *Ian Webber collection*

A fine view of Burford, between Oxford and Cheltenham, in May 1931. Pausing on its journey towards Cheltenham is L54 (DG 770), one of the London Lorries-bodied Leyland TS2s delivered during the previous year. This location is still easily recognisable more than 70 years on!
John Aldridge collection

An unusual view over the inspection pits at Cheltenham in 1934. On the left is L53 (DG 769), a London Lorries-bodied Leyland TS2 of 1930, whilst the centre vehicle is all-Leyland TS2 L34 (DF 8391); the right-hand coach is a Wycombe-bodied Gilford 168OT, No G65 (DG 1913). Note the offside toilet compartments on the two Leylands, the windows on L53 appearing more ornate with leaded lights. Note too, the access to the luggage racks on the roofs, by ladder on L34 but by foot-holes on the later vehicles.
John Aldridge collection

The vehicles

The first deliveries of 1930 were split between Gilford and Leyland. Nos G41-50 (DG 92/4, 484-7, 548/9, 765/6) were London Lorries-bodied Gilford 168SDs, while L51-60 (DG 767-76) were more Leyland Tiger TS2s, also with London Lorries bodywork. Both batches were withdrawn by the end of the decade. These TS2s were the last to be bought new, and the last new Gilfords followed in 1931 in the shape of G61-6 (DG 1909-14), Wycombe-bodied 168OTs. Until 1936 the only other vehicles to be bought new were a quartet of little Leyland Cubs, used mainly for tour work; lasting until only 1940, L70-3 (DG 6557-60) were Duple-bodied KP3s and seated 20.

The various takeovers by Black & White accounted for most of the acquisitions during the mid-'Thirties, although few were retained for long. An unusual addition to the fleet in 1932 was A14 (MT 2042), a Strachan & Brown-bodied Albion PNC26 which came from F. J. Webb of Street in Somerset, although that company was not acquired; new in 1929, it was probably a former Albion demonstrator and was withdrawn in 1937. With the takeover of Ensign in 1932 came G67 (MY 4210), a Gilford 168OT, and a variety of cars, while the acquisition in 1933 of Link Safety Coaches brought a trio of Studebakers, a Chevrolet and a pair of useful Leyland Tigers. The Leylands were L68 (RU 9873), a TS2, and L69 (LJ 2106), a TS3, their original bodies (believed to have been Leylands) being removed and sold locally for £12 10s (£12.50) the pair; the chassis were rebodied by Duple and as such lasted until 1951.

South Wales Express Coaches had bought a collection of AEC Regals, a couple of Gilfords and an AJS Pilot. This operator was acquired jointly with Red & White Services and its fleet divided, Black & White being left with two Gilford 168OTs and two AEC Regals, the last of which had gone by 1937; one of the Regals, Metal Bodies-bodied A77 (PJ 5777), appeared for a while in publicity.

From 1936 until 1949 Black & White favoured Bristol chassis, the first, B78-85 (BAD 631-8), being JO6Gs with Burlingham bodies (of which B79 was badly damaged in the air-raid on Cheltenham in 1940 and received a new Duple body, at a cost of £805). Further JO6Gs, this time with ECW bodies, arrived in 1937 as B86-93 (CDD 1-6, 8, 11). Bristol's successor to the J was the L, Black & White's first examples being B94-9 (CDG 371-6), L6Gs with ECW bodies, delivered in 1938. The 1939 intake consisted of B100-5 (DDF 44-9), L6Gs bodied by

▲ G44 (DG 485), one of the 1930 delivery of normal-control Gilford 168SDs with London Lorries 26-seat coachwork. They were withdrawn from the fleet during 1937/8. *Author's collection*

▲ A14 (MT 2042), the Albion PNC26 with Strachan & Brown 26-seat bodywork acquired from F. J. Webb of Street, Somerset, in 1932. Withdrawn in 1937 it ended up with Oxfordshire operator Worth's of Enstone. *Ian Webber collection*

Two Black & White coaches receive attention at Cheltenham in the early 1930s. On the left is Gilford 168OT/Wycombe G63 (DG 1911) with bonnet up, whilst undergoing refuelling and a tyre check is Leyland TS2/London Lorries L55 (DG 771).The position of the toilet can again be seen on the TS2, determined by the decorative offside windows.
John Aldridge collection

A77 (PJ 5777), one of the vehicles taken over with South Wales Express Coaches, London, in 1933. A 1932 AEC Regal with Metal Bodies coachwork, it lasted only a few years with Black & White, being withdrawn in 1936, but saw further service until at least 1949. Sister Regal A76 (GN 4289) fared rather better; following withdrawal in 1937 it served with a variety of operators, surviving into the early 1960s.
Ian Webber collection

A fine official view of B86 (CDD 1), the first of the 1937 Bristol JO6Gs with Eastern Coach Works 30-seat bodies. These vehicles cost the company a little over £1,081 apiece. *ECW archives / S. J. Butler collection*

An interior view of B86, looking forward. *ECW archives / S. J. Butler collection*

Duple — a combination repeated in 1940 with B106-8 (EDD 460-2). The influx of Bristols led to the demise of the prewar stock, except a few of the Tigers.

The first new vehicles to enter the fleet after the war were more Bristol L6Gs with Duple bodywork. B109-18 (HDD 652-61) were new in 1948 and lasted 12 years in the fleet. Ten further Bristol L6Gs, B119-28 (JDD 490-9), followed in 1949; bodywork was again by Duple, although this batch was distinctive in having full fronts (as opposed to half-cabs) — an arrangement popular at the time as a means of creating a more modern appearance.

With the prevailing shortage of new vehicles, and with Bristol vehicles now available only to state-owned companies (Bristol Tramways' 40% share presumably being insufficient for Black & White to qualify), two batches of second-hand coaches were acquired in 1950. From South Wales Transport came 59-67, 70/1 (BWN 315-24 and DHA 800), Dennis Lancet IIs with Dennis bodies, new in 1938/9, while from City of Oxford came Weymann-bodied AEC Regals 72-7 (EFC 294-9), by then 14 years old. Both batches were withdrawn at the end of the 1951 summer season, along with L68/9, the last two prewar Leyland Tigers.

In 1951, with Bristols denied it, Black & White returned to Leyland for 20 Royal Tiger PSU1/11 chassis — the fleet's first underfloor-engined coaches — with Willowbrook bodies. Centre entrances were specified — an arrangement that remained a standard feature for 10 years. Nos L129-48 were registered KDF 980-99, half having sliding roofs — a throwback to prewar days. Another 11 Royal Tigers, again with Willowbrook bodywork — L149-59 (LDD 990-9, MDF 484) — arrived at Cheltenham in 1952/3.

In 1954 there was another change of chassis and body supplier with the intake of G160-75 (NDG 160-75). These were examples of the Guy Arab LUF — a lighter-weight version of the UF — and were bodied by Duple to that firm's 'Elizabethan' design. A further batch of LUFs followed in 1955, although bodywork reverted to Willowbrook; these were G176-87 (PAD 176-87). The delivery of the Guys allowed the withdrawal of the 1936/7 Bristol JO6Gs, B78-93. The summer of 1954 also saw the hiring of 15 SOS/English Electric coaches from Midland Red.

A final half-dozen Willowbrook-bodied Guy Arab LUFs, G188-93 (SAD 188-93) were bought in 1956, along with the company's first AEC Reliance, A194 (SDF 194), which was exhibited by Willowbrook at the 1956 Commercial Motor Show. The Reliance/Willowbrook combination was favoured for the 1957 intake, A195-203 (SDF 195-203). Correspondingly, out of the fleet in 1956/7 went all but two of the last prewar Bristols.

Six AEC Regals with Weymann bodies were also used as a stopgap during 1950/1; at least four are seen here, including EFC 296/9.
East Pennine Transport Group

A number of acquired vehicles entered the fleet in 1950, which year represented something of a watershed for Black & White: it had bought its last Bristols in 1949 and would turn to underfloor-engined chassis in 1951. Here, in the company of a Midland Red SOS SLR, one of the ex-South Wales Transport Dennis Lancet IIs, BWN 324, waits on relief duties, with another behind.
Mike Greenwood collection

The new age dawns! Three of the 1951 Willowbrook-bodied Leyland Royal Tigers line up over the pits towards the end of their first season of service.
John Aldridge collection

Leyland Royal Tiger L129 (KDF 980) sweeps through Hounslow during 1951 on a Gloucester–London Victoria working — a journey that would take a little over five hours.
John Aldridge collection

The combination of Guy Arab LUF chassis
and Willowbrook bodywork was chosen
for deliveries in 1955/6, totalling some 18
vehicles. G183 (PAD 183) dated from 1956
and was probably not very old when seen
working the Cheltenham to Nottingham/
Mansfield route. Note the destination board
— not a standard feature on a Black &
White coach. *Author's collection*

▲ Willowbrook was also favoured in 1956/7 for a batch of 10
AEC Reliances, all of which featured in this contemporary
advertisement *John Aldridge collection*

G191 (SAD 191), one of the 1956 Arab LUFs, heads away from Cheltenham towards Bournemouth on the 2pm departure in May 1957. On the extreme left can be seen the new office block, opened the previous year.
John Aldridge

A hand-coloured print of A194 (SDF 194), the AEC Reliance exhibited by Willowbrook at the 1956 Commercial Motor Show.
Ian Webber collection

An interesting trio over the inspection pits at Cheltenham in 1957. Taking centre stage is 1954 Guy Arab LUF/Duple G167(NDG 167), whilst parked on the right is 1952 Leyland Royal Tiger/ Willowbrook L149 (LDD 990). The vehicle on the left is Ribble Leyland Tiger Cub/ Burlingham 969 (JRN 35), which has arrived on an X24 service from Liverpool.
John Aldridge

A204 (WDG 630), the first of the Roe Dalesman-bodied AEC Reliances, was entered in the British Coach Rally at Brighton in April 1959. These were the only vehicles delivered in the 1951-61 period not to feature the centre entrance/exit layout. *Mike Sutcliffe*

It was the custom for Black & White to hire in coaches from Midland Red to work express services at busy periods, thus allowing its better vehicles to fulfil private-hire and tour commitments. In 1959 ten 20-year-old SOS ONCs with Duple bodies, temporarily numbered MR1-10, were received on loan during the summer; five are lined up awaiting further duties on 14 June. *Mike Sutcliffe*

There were no new coaches in 1958, and just five more AEC Reliances arrived in 1959, notably carrying Roe Dalesman bodywork, as A204-8 (WDG 630-4). Further Midland Red coaches were hired for the 1959 season, these being 10 Duple-bodied SOS ONCs celebrating their 20th year. Over the same period yet more Bristols left the fleet — B104/5 in 1958 and B106-8 in 1959.

New coaches delivered in 1960 and, indeed, 1961 consisted of more AEC Reliances, this time bodied by a third coachbuilder — Duple, with its 'Britannia' model — although the centre entrance/exit continued to be specified. The 1960 batch of eight were numbered A209-16 (4209-16 AD), the first four initially seating 37 for touring work, the others 41. The 1961 intake of six were A217-22 (8217-22 AD) — all 37-seaters until 1970, when all except A217 (withdrawn with accident damage in 1969) were re-seated to 41. The new arrivals saw the withdrawal of the last of the Bristols — B109-18 in 1960 and B119-28 in 1961.

For 1962 and 1963 there was a return to Leyland, this time the Leopard PSU3 chassis — Black & White's first 36ft coaches, and amongst the first anywhere in the UK — underneath 47-seat Plaxton Panorama bodywork. The 1962 batch were numbered L223-31 (6773-81 DD), whilst those delivered in 1963 were

L232-41 (4872-81 DF). More Leyland Leopards were delivered in 1964, again bodied by Plaxton, as L242-6 (AAD 242-6B). However, a final appearance by the AEC Reliance, at least for new deliveries, saw the arrival of A247-51 (AAD 247-51B), which carried the first Harrington bodies, in this case Cavaliers, for Black & White. For 1965 there were further Harringtons — Grenadiers — on Leyland Leopards L252-6 (DDG 252-6C), while L257-61 (DDG 257-61C) received Duple (Northern) Commander bodies.

Although 1966 saw the familiar pattern of the arrival of more Leyland Leopards in the shape of Plaxton Panorama-bodied L262-8 (HDG 362-8D), the year's other arrival caused rather more of a stir.

The early 1960s saw a swing towards high-capacity single-deckers in place of double-deckers for bus work — a development which led the major manufacturers to introduce a number of high-powered rear-engined chassis designs. Daimler had built a couple of prototype chassis in 1961, with an initial sale (to PMT) in 1964. The potential of the Roadliner, as the chassis was called, for coaching was realised early on by Black & White, which received D272 (HDG 772D) in 1966; indeed, both

▲ London Victoria in 1960. Working the Cheltenham service is a brand-
new Duple-bodied AEC Reliance A213 (4213 AD), one of the first batch
of vehicles with reversed registrations. Edging in on the left is East Kent
GFN 273, a 1952 Beadle-Leyland. *John Aldridge*

Black & White's first 36ft coaches were nine Plaxton Panorama-bodied Leyland Leopards delivered in 1962. No L227 is seen on layover at Portsmouth in the late 1960s. *Photobus*

An almost monochrome 1960s scene is relieved by Midland Red double-deckers at Leicester. Black & White Leyland Leopard/Plaxton L228 (4878 DF) has just arrived from Cheltenham via Coventry. *Photobus*

Derby bus station was built in the 1930s and 70 years later is under threat of closure and demolition. In happier times, AEC Reliance/Harrington A250 (AAD 250B) has just unloaded on arrival from Cheltenham in the mid-1960s. *Roy Marshall / Photobus*

A 1960s view of AEC Reliance/Harrington A249 (AAD 249B) pausing at Leicester *en route* from Nottingham and Cheltenham. *Mike Sutcliffe*

Seven years separate these two coaches at Oxford. Black & White Leyland Royal Tiger/Willowbrook L139 (KDF 990) of 1951 is beginning to look a little dated alongside Royal Blue Bristol MW6G/ECW 2229 (XUO 712) of 1958. They are bound for Southampton and Bournemouth respectively. *Mike Greenwood collection*

The first 36ft coaches looked impressive when compared with what had gone before. Plaxton-bodied Leyland Leopard L228 (6778 DD) is seen loading for Cheltenham at London Victoria when new. *John Aldridge collection*

The last Bristols in the fleet before the RELHs were the 1949 Burlingham-bodied L6Gs, withdrawn after the 1961 season; B123 (JDD 494) hadn't long to serve when seen at London Victoria that August. It looked to be still in good condition (although both 'Bristol' badge and scroll are missing from the radiator), but apparently no further owner was found for B123 after sale to dealer North, Sherburn-in-Elmet. *R. A. Jenkinson/ Geoff Mills collection*

EAST KENT

PRESTON (KENT)		ASHFORD (KENT)	OSTENDE
SEASALTER		SELLINDGE	AMSTERDAM
WHITSTABLE		HYTHE	BRUSSELS
TANKERTON		SANDGATE	COLOGNE
SWALECLIFFE		FOLKESTONE	FRANKFURT
HERNE BAY	LYDD (FERRYFIELD AIRPORT)	DOVER	AND OTHER EUROFABUS CONNECTIONS VIA DOVER

11

ASSOCIATED MOTORWAYS	YORKSHIRE SERVICES	EASTERN NATIONAL	WESTCLIFF
CHELTENHAM	DONCASTER	COLCHESTER	BASILDON
GLOUCESTER	LEEDS	CLACTON	HADLEIGH (ESSEX)
ROSS-ON-WYE	HARROGATE	JAYWICK SANDS	LEIGH-ON-SEA
ABERYSTWYTH	SHEFFIELD	ALL DEPARTURES FOR ABOVE SERVICE WILL LEAVE FROM	WESTCLIFF-ON-SEA
CARDIFF	BRADFORD		SOUTHEND-ON-SEA
SWANSEA	KEIGHLEY		ALL DEPARTURES FOR ABOVE DESTINATIONS WILL LEAVE FROM BAY 12
SOUTH & WEST WALES	HULL		

12

EXIT LANES

ASSOCIATED MOTORWAYS   CHELTENHAM SPA

BLACK & WHITE MOTORWAYS

Panorama

6778 DD

Chief Engineer Arthur Gorton and General Manager Leslie Grimmett were involved in its development. Exhibited at the Earls Court Show, where it created plenty of interest, doubtless to the delight of the Daimler sales staff, D272 was an SRC6 model, powered by a Cummins V6 engine, and carried Plaxton Panorama bodywork. The interior was well appointed, and its black and white decor complimented the exterior. It was also the first coach in the fleet to feature semi-automatic transmission.

Further Roadliners were included in the 1967 intake, D273-9 (KDD 273-9E) being bodied similarly by Plaxton and fitted with Cummins engines. No D276, with 44 (rather than 47) seats, was declared Coach of the Year at a wet Blackpool — the first major award by a THC or BET entry — and later received the same accolade at a rather sunnier Brighton. Other 1967 deliveries consisted of 13 Plaxton-bodied Leyland Leopard PSU3s — L269-71 (HDG 369-71D) and L280-9 (KDD 280-9E); L269-71 were actually built in 1966 but held at Plaxtons over the winter.

On the debit side, 1966 saw the demise of the 1954 batch of Guy Arab LUFs, while those dating from 1955/6 went in 1967/8

respectively, the latter year also witnessing the withdrawal of the first AEC Reliances.

Regrettably the Cummins engines fitted to early Roadliners proved notoriously problematic in service, and in 1968 D272 was re-engined by Daimler with a Perkins V8, which it would retained until withdrawal. Despite the type's poor reliability, all deliveries in 1968/9 (and, indeed, 1970) were of Daimler Roadliners with Plaxton bodies. Nos D290-9 (NAD 290-9F) had Cummins engines, but the 1969 batch, Panorama Elite-bodied D300-9 (RDG 300-9G), were SRP8 models featuring the slightly superior Perkins unit.

For the record, the fleet at the turn of 1969/70 stood at 112 vehicles — AEC Reliance/Willowbrook 198-203, AEC Reliance/Roe 204-8, AEC Reliance/Duple 209-22, Leyland Leopard/Plaxton 223-46/62-71/80-9, AEC Reliance/Harrington 247-51, Leyland Leopard/Harrington 252-6, Leyland Leopard/Duple Northern 257-61 and Daimler Roadliner/ Plaxton 272-9/90-309; at that time, 307/8 were on loan to Western National and 309 was on loan to Devon General.

By the mid-1960s the 1952 batch of LDD-registered Willowbrook-bodied Leyland Royal Tigers were reaching the end of their time with Black & White; two were withdrawn in 1965, the rest following in 1966. In its last few months, L156 (LDD 997) pauses at Bedford bus station *en route* from Cheltenham to Great Yarmouth — a service that dates back to 1952, although initially it ran only as far as Cambridge. Note the destinations painted in whitewash on the fourth window: Brackley, Buckingham and Bedford. *J. A. Maris*

Also withdrawn *en masse* in 1966 were G160-75, the 1954 Guy Arab LUF/Duples, to be replaced by Leyland Leopards and Daimler Roadliners. Cheltenham-bound from Nottingham, G172 (NDG 172) waits in the bleak surroundings of St Margaret's bus station, Leicester, on a windswept day in the early 1960s. *Mike Sutcliffe*

The first Harrington-bodied coaches for the Black & White fleet came in 1964, towards the end of production for this manufacturer. AEC Reliances A247-51 (AAD 247-51B) were used on tour work for some years, and A247/8 are seen thus engaged when new. The former is waiting to take up one of the many different Cotswold Villages tours, while the latter is set for a theatre visit, perhaps Oxford, Coventry, Stratford or Bristol. *Edward G. Hodgkins*

Brand-new A250 (AAD 250B) is seen here on Associated Motorways work, however. Awaiting a driver at Cheltenham in May 1964, the 'Bristol Only' written in whitewash on the first window suggests a duplicate or short working. *Author's collection*

The other Harrington-bodied coaches in the fleet were on Leyland Leopard chassis. L255 (DDG 255C) was one of the five, new in 1965, and is seen in July of that year on tour duties in Kenilworth Road, Coventry. *T. W. Moore*

Duple Northern-bodied Leyland Leopards were delivered alongside the last of the Harringtons. No L261 (DDG 261C) leaves Cheltenham for Torquay in the late 1960s. *Author's collection*

Another of the 1965 batch of Duple Commander-bodied Leopards, L257 (DDG 257C) loads at Cheltenham for Torquay in 1969 alongside a Wolverhampton-bound Midland Red BMMO C5, No 4786 (786 GHA). *V. C. Jones*

The first Daimler Roadliner was D272 (HDG 772D), new in 1966, and further deliveries followed until 1970. Cummins-engined D276 (KDD 276E) was fairly new when loading at London Victoria for Gloucester in 1967. This particular vehicle was entered at the 1967 Brighton and Blackpool coach rallies and won Coach of the Year at both. *Ian Allan Library*

Rear view of Roadliner D277 (KDD 277E), showing the multiplicity of ventilation grilles. *Ian Allan Library*

The distinctive rear-end profiles of Plaxton-bodied Daimler Roadliners D298/3/4/7 (NAD 298/3/4/7F) parked at Cheltenham *c*1969. *Arnold Richardson / Photobus*

Ten Daimler Roadliner SRC6/Plaxton coaches constituted the 1968 intake. About a year old when seen at Exeter in the summer of 1969, D294 (NAD 294F) enjoys a 30min refreshment break on the 11.00am limited-stop Saturdays-only working from Paignton to Derby (not via Cheltenham).
Author's collection

Wet day at Llandudno! Daimler Roadliner D304 (RDG 304G), one of the later deliveries of the type, with Perkins V8 engines, waits in the rain to return home.
G. H. F. Atkins

3. Decline and Demise — Into the 1970s and Beyond

In 1965 Barbara Castle was appointed Minister of Transport in Harold Wilson's Labour Government. She was given the green light to proceed with a long-held dream, namely that of an integrated transport system. The plan, as far as the bus companies outside the conurbations were concerned, was to merge the BET and THC interests into one. Agreement was finally reached in November 1967, resulting in its inclusion in the 1968 Transport Act, and the new National Bus Company (NBC) commenced operation on 1 January 1969. Coaching operations now became the responsibility of the Central Activities Group. Initially, only those fleets operating just coaches, such as Black & White, came under CAG control, although in time (1973) the coaches of the other subsidiaries came into the National Travel fold.

As far as Black & White was concerned, there was initially little change — Associated Motorways carried on as before, with new joint services commencing during 1969. From 11 October 1970, however, the practice of reallocating routes each summer and winter between member companies generally came to an end. With all operators now coming NBC control, it was decided to give responsibility for each group of services to a single operator, on a geographical basis. For Black & White this meant destinations towards London, the South West and the Midlands — its old area, in fact — but this did not sit well with everybody. In Birmingham, for instance, Digbeth coach station was picketed by Midland Red coach drivers over the transfer to Black & White of the Birmingham–Paignton service, which they had operated since the 1930s.

The livery did change however, with a simpler application — the black was limited to a broad waistband with a white 'BLACK & WHITE' fleetname ('MOTORWAYS' being dropped). The winds of change would soon ruffle more than a few feathers, however; as the motorway network was extended, it was realised that faster times could be achieved by avoiding Cheltenham, and a mini-interchange was established at Aust Services ('Motorport' in some timetables) at the Severn Bridge

on the M4, allowing connections between South Wales and destinations in the South and West of England.

The NBC regional liveries proved to be short-lived and were gradually replaced by an all-over white scheme, with 'N A T I O N A L' applied in alternate red and blue letters. Initially, fleetnames were very small, almost to the point of being unreadable, and positioned over the front wheel-arches. It was then underlined by an appropriate colour — black, in the case of Black & White. These tiny fleetnames seemed to be a grudging acknowledgement of the past identities. Larger fleetnames were later restored, albeit in red, but at least one could now see at a glance which company actually operated a particular vehicle. This, of course, was all part of the corporate image, the 'branding' of a national network where individuality was discouraged. A unified route-numbering system was duly established (services in the South West being numbered in the 6xx and 7xx series), and by the mid-1970s the late Frederick

Wood, Chairman of NBC, had seen his vision of an American Greyhound-style network realised.

On 11 February 1974 Black & White Motorways was renamed National Travel (South West), with the Associated Motorways pool ceasing at the same time, with most licences passing to the new company. (That said, as late as 1975 former Associated Motorways services were indicated as such in the summer NTSW timetable book.) National Travel (South West) was also responsible for three other National Travel subsidiaries — Exeter-based Greenslades Tours, Wessex Coaches of Bristol and Shamrock & Rambler, operating from Bournemouth. Greenslades' history can be traced back to 1912, when local excursions were operated; the business grew and became part

of the BET group in 1953 and was co-ordinated with Devon General's Grey Cars before merging with the latter. Wessex Coaches of Bristol, operating tours and excursions as well as a large contract fleet, was placed under NBC control from August 1974 as Wessex National. Shamrock & Rambler Motor Coaches had been taken over by the Transport Holding Co in 1966 and thus passed into NBC ownership in 1969.

The four fleets retained their separate identities, with Black & White, Wessex National, Greenslades and Shamrock & Rambler fleetnames being retained on vehicles generally employed on tour and excursion work; South West fleetnames were intended for vehicles used on express services, although in practice any vehicle would be pressed into service, regardless of fleetname!

In the early 1970s Hereford saw Associated Motorways services into Cheltenham from various parts of Wales. However, there is nothing in this July 1970 view of Leyland Leopard/Plaxton L231 (6781 DD) to indicate where this working originated. The coach looks a little bare, having lost both its winged Black & White motif over the front dome and Leyland Leopard badge from its nose. *John Jones*

Leyland Leopard/Plaxton L283 (KDD 283E) pulls away from the bus station at Hereford *en route* from South Wales to Cheltenham on 18 July 1970. *John Jones*

▲ The new Black & White NBC image, displayed on Bristol RELH/
Plaxton 330 (ADG 330K), wearing the livery in which it was delivered.
The coach is working a half-day tour from Gloucester and Cheltenham
to the Benedictine Abbey at Prinknash, which in 1973 would have cost
all of 40p! *Photobus*

Plaxton-bodied Leyland Leopards provide a contrast in livery styles at Oxford in February 1971. L236 (4876 DF) wears the more traditional style, while L230 (6780 DD) sports the early NBC image. *M. D. Shaw*

An early-1970s view at Cheltenham, with a selection of Black & White and Red & White coaches ready for the 'off'. The old 'BLACK & WHITE MOTORWAYS LTD' sign has been replaced by a simple 'NATIONAL' and logo, although a smaller 'BLACK & WHITE' has appeared in place of 'COACH STATION' on the far left of the canopy. *John Aldridge collection*

Duple Northern-bodied Leyland Leopard L261 (DDG 261C) carried the full black waistband but retained the old-style fleetname, when caught in the sunshine in Castle Street, Salisbury, on its way down to Portsmouth from Bristol on 10 April 1971. *Philip Wallis*

The early National livery is illustrated here by Leyland Leopard L320 (YDF 320K), leaving Cheltenham for South Wales in February 1973. The black underlining is as deep as the fleetname itself! *John Jones*

▲ Also wearing the early National livery is Daimler Roadliner D302 (RDG 302G), seen receiving a wash and brush-up at Cheltenham in February 1973. *John Jones*

Loading at Cheltenham for Nottingham *c*1975, at the start of a route long associated with Black & White, is Leyland Leopard/Duple Northern L260 (DDG 260C). *Author's collection*

Black & White Coach Tour ticket and envelope, 1973

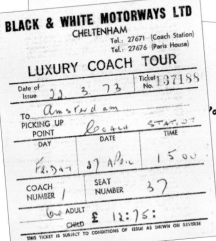

The mid-1970s still saw Black & White coaches travelling far and wide. Summer Saturday departures would actually begin at 02.30, as overnight services arriving from the north headed out to South Wales and the West Country. In some cases a Black & White driver would take over from an inbound working, taking the vehicle to its destination. One such was the Fridays-only 19.00 Glasgow–Paignton (service 920), which arrived at Cheltenham at 02.00 on the Saturday morning, worked by a Western SMT Leyland Leopard/Alexander Y-type; this would leave Cheltenham at 02.30, arriving at Paignton at 06.58 and returning as the 09.30 for Glasgow and reaching Cheltenham at 14.00, when the Black & White driver would be relieved; the Western SMT driver would then leave at 14.30, to arrive back at Glasgow at 21.30. The first of the London services would leave as early as 04.00, but the next clutch of connecting services would be at 08.30, leaving for South Wales, the Midlands, Bournemouth and London. The next busy time was 11.30, with departures to such as Barry, Minehead, Margate, Portsmouth, Great Yarmouth and Blackpool. At 14.30 would come the main activity of the day, as services that had left early in the day from

◄ During the 1970s Black & White operated several contracts in the Cheltenham area, and these provided the company with useful work, particularly during the winter months. However, it must have run out of vehicles on 7 July 1978, when Eastern Scottish Bristol RELH/Alexander ZA191 (EWS 191D) was used on a run to Cleeve School, Bishops Cleeve! The vehicle would have arrived at Cheltenham on a 657 from Edinburgh. *Colin Martin*

either north or west converged on Cheltenham. The 640 from Aberystwyth, for example, would have left at 08.45 to arrive at Cheltenham at 14.00, allowing homeward-bound holidaymakers to connect with a number of services north. In the opposite direction, steelworkers from Scunthorpe heading for the West Country would have left on service 659 at 06.50 to reach Cheltenham at 14.05, with a variety of destinations to choose from at 14.30 — perhaps the 721 to Ilfracombe (to arrive at 19.00) or the 730 to Paignton (arriving at 20.41). The next departure time was 16.30, with coaches heading mainly north, while the last mass departure would be at 18.30, for the Midlands and London. (There were later departures, mostly to London, but this gives a flavour of the scene at Cheltenham at this time.)

In between these periods of activity vehicles would be serviced, refuelled and cleaned, with visiting coaches being accommodated before returning home. Indeed, drivers had 'spare' duties specifically for moving vehicles around the coach station but while so employed might be called upon to fill in for another driver or work a duplicate; in some cases, particularly during the summer months, a Black & White driver would be asked to relieve a driver from another company and would thus gain

experience of unfamiliar vehicle types, such as a manual-gearbox dual-purpose Bristol RELH/ECW (Eastern Counties) or, more exotic, a Seddon VII/Alexander (Eastern Scottish).

An interesting addition to the destinations available from Cheltenham was Paris, accessible from 6 August 1976. The application for the licence, made some time previously, was the first for an express service by Black & White in its own right since the formation of Associated Motorways. The inaugural journey, numbered 777, left Cheltenham at 17.30 worked by Leopard/Duple 110, travelling via Bristol, Bath, Salisbury and Southampton. The Channel was crossed, appropriately, by Normandy Ferries' *Leopard*, arrival at Le Havre being at 06.50 local time, and Paris (Place de la Madeleine) was eventually reached at 10.30. Black & White drivers were no strangers to driving abroad, as Continental tours were already well established. Unfortunately, however, the drivers' uniform upset the French authorities; being black with white piping and featuring the company emblem on lapels as well as on the peaked cap, this was uncomfortably close to that worn by the SS during the Nazi occupation during World War 2 and was subsequently changed to one of light grey.

NBC Black & White Tours brochure 1973.

National Travel Coach Parties handbook, 1976.

The first Cheltenham–Paris service under the auspices of National Travel (South West) ran on 7 August 1976. Leyland Leopard 110 (PDD 110M) worked the service and is seen here on arrival at the Place de la Madeleine. *P. Ormerod*

The Paris service was later extended into Wales as service 778; Leyland Leopard/Duple 192 (AFH 192T) loads at Cardiff on 26 June 1979. *John Jones*

National Express map from the early 1980s, showing services connecting as the 15.00 Cheltenham Interchange.

How to find us in Cheltenham

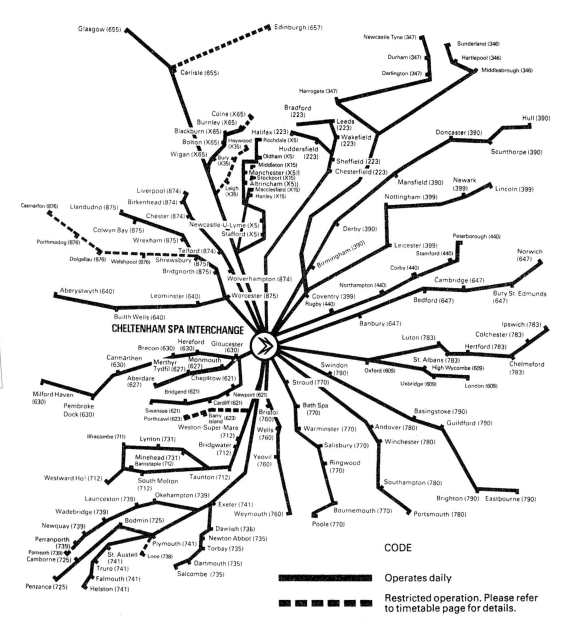

CODE

▬▬▬▬ Operates daily

▬ ▬ ▬ ▬ Restricted operation. Please refer to timetable page for details.

The vehicles

As was mentioned in the previous chapter, the only new coaches to be delivered in 1970 were further Daimler Roadliners — Perkins-engined SRP8s — although Plaxton Panorama Elite-bodied D310-9 (UAD 310-9H) turned out to be the last of their type to enter the fleet, as vehicle policy would henceforth come increasingly under centralised NBC control; they also were the last vehicles to be delivered wearing the traditional Black & White livery. The first loans for some years were of four Bristol MW6G dual-purpose vehicles from Bristol which helped out during August and September. Withdrawn in 1970 were various AEC Reliances from the 1957, 1959, 1960 and 1961 batches. (This included the five Roe-bodied Reliances, A204-8; A204-7 were sold as runners for £500 each, whereas accident-damaged A208 managed to fetch £660!)

Eight more Daimler Roadliners should have appeared in 1971, but the order, no doubt to the relief of many, was cancelled, the vehicles being exported to South Africa instead. It was back to the old and familiar in the shape of L320-9 (YDF 320-9K) — more Plaxton-bodied Leyland Leopards. Also in 1971 there arrived the first secondhand vehicles since 1950, in the shape of 140-3 (140-3 DBO), Duple (Northern) Continental-bodied Leyland Leopards new to Western Welsh in 1963. From the same source came four Harrington-bodied AEC Reliances (ABO 146-9B), loaned during August and September. The last of the Duple-bodied AEC Reliances were delicensed at the end of the 1971 summer season, but more significant was the withdrawal of Roadliners D273-9, all despatched to dealer Martin's of Weaverham, after just four years in the fleet.

The replacements for the cancelled Daimler Roadliners were, perhaps surprisingly, Bristol RELH6Gs with Plaxton Panorama Elite II bodywork, numbered 330-6 (ADG 330-6K); ordered by Western National and built in 1970, they were bodied in 1971 and licensed in 1972. Two demonstrators were received during December 1972 — UOO 661L, a Duple-bodied Ford R226, and YXE 844H, a Duple-bodied Bedford YRQ. The following year saw further Leyland Leopards — 337-46 (FDF 337-46L) — enter the fleet, but, for the first time, bodywork was by Duple; perhaps more significantly, these were the first coaches to be delivered in white National coach livery. One vehicle — Bristol RELH / Plaxton EHW 315K — operated on loan from Bristol in August and September. The 1968 batch of Daimler Roadliners all went to a dealer in May or July, while older vehicles to leave

the fleet in 1973 were various 1962/3 Leopards and 1964 AEC Reliances A247-51.

The 1974 intake consisted of another 13 Leyland Leopard PSU3s, 100-12 (PDD 100-11M, PDG 112M), all but 112 with Duple Dominant coachwork; the odd man out had a Plaxton Panorama Elite III body, having been diverted new from Greenslades in exchange for Black & White Bristol RELH/Plaxton 330. Further second-hand coaches entering the fleet in 1974 were 230/1, Plaxton Panorama Elite-bodied Leyland Leopards acquired from Greenslades; registered YTX 322/3H, these had originated with Rhondda Transport in 1970. Out of the fleet — to Greenslades — went the rest of the RELH/Plaxtons and three more of the 1962 Leopards.

In November 1974 National Travel (South West) instituted a renumbering scheme that brought together the four operating divisions. Black & White vehicles were numbered in the range 100-249, only the Leopards delivered earlier in the year, 100-12, retaining their old numbers.

No new vehicles were bought in 1975, but a number of Duple (Northern)-bodied Leyland Leopards were acquired: from

▲ In a little-known occurrence early in 1973, a trio of ex-Southdown Harrington-bodied Leyland Leopard L2s (8740-2 CD) were sent to Cheltenham from Tillings. They were not well received, however, and were sold almost immediately to Grey-Green. Although they stayed long enough to have 'BLACK & WHITE' applied to the glass below the rear window, they probably did not do any work for the company. *Colin Martin*

The old order at Leicester, with Roe-bodied AEC Reliance A204 (WDG 630) in traditional livery on loan to Midland Red in February 1970. This was its final year with Black & White, the entire batch having been withdrawn by the end of the season. *Omnicolour*

▼ Bristol RELH/Plaxton 334 (ADG 334K) stands at Cheltenham in February 1973. Having entered service early in 1972, all seven of the batch (diverted from Western National) would pass to either Greenslades or Wessex National in 1974, before being reunited in the enlarged National Travel (South West) fleet in 1978. *John Jones*

◀

The 1967 intake consisted of 13 Leyland Leopard PSU3s and seven Daimler Roadliner SRC6s, all with Plaxton bodywork. One of the Leylands, L284 (KDD 284E), is seen at London Victoria in March 1976, by which time it had been renumbered 184.
Charles Dean / Author's collection

Further coaches acquired in 1975 were a trio of Duple Northern-bodied Leyland Leopards from National Travel (South East) but which had been new to Samuelsons New Transport Co in 1969. With a full load, 190 (XVB 466G) arrives at Cheltenham on service 488 from Grimsby via Lincoln, Market Harborough and Stratford-upon-Avon — a journey of nearly seven hours. Many of the passengers would doubtless have been travelling further west on one of the 14.30 departures; Torquay, for instance, would not be reached until 18.29, and Helston not until 21.50 — a long day! Amongst the vehicles in the coach station is an Eastern Scottish Seddon awaiting departure on an Edinburgh-bound 637. *John Jones* ▶

◀◀ The seven Plaxton-bodied Bristol RELHs that entered service in 1972 were replacements for a cancelled order for Daimler Roadliners. When nearly new, 335 (ADG 335K) swings out of Cheltenham bound for Llandudno via Hereford, Shrewsbury and Rhyl — a journey that would take almost seven hours. *John Aldridge collection*

◀ The Daimler Roadliners unfortunately had a very short working life with Black & White. This shot of 207 and 204 (RDG 307/4G) taken in May 1976 could perhaps have been taken in a coach park; in fact, both vehicles are withdrawn, stored at Willowbrook's premises at Loughborough on behalf of dealer TPE of Macclesfield. Indeed, the whole batch of 10, along with 210-9 (UAD 310-9H) were here from November 1975, all eventually finding new owners. *Geoff Mills*

National Travel (South East) came 190-2 (XVB 466-8G), with Commander IV coachwork, while Midland Red provided Commanders 203-5/10-2/4/5/7/8 (CHA 93-5, 105/6/9/13/5/7/8C). Withdrawals included, significantly, the last of the Daimler Roadliners — all 20 from the 1969/70 batches — as well as the remainder of the 1962 Leopards.

The year 1976 saw yet more Leopards, by now an NBC standard; 113-20 (MDF 113-20P) carried Duple Dominant bodies. However, 150-60 (NDF 150-60P) were Duple-bodied AEC Reliances, of which 157-60 were the company's first 12m coaches. Yet more ex-Midland Red Duple (Northern) Leyland Leopard PSU3s received were 196-200/6/7/9/13/9 (CHA 75/9-81/3, 96/8, 100/12/9C); from Southdown came a pair of PSU3s with Plaxton Panorama bodies, 193/4 (EUF 191/4D), whilst Ribble supplied 232-6 (KCK 979-83H), predictably more Leopards, this time of the shorter (33ft) PSU4

variety, with Plaxton Panorama Elite bodywork seating just 36. A further eight ex-Southdown PSU3 Leopard/ Plaxtons, — mentioned here as they were licensed initially to National Travel (South West) — were placed in the Wessex fleet, while a trio of AEC Reliances with Duple Commander IV bodies, 147-9 (UWN 67H, RCY 55/6H), were acquired from South Wales Transport.

From 1977 until the end of the decade, new deliveries were Leyland Leopards of various types with bodywork by Willowbrook (Spacecar) or Plaxton (Supreme), the exceptions being a pair of Duple Dominant II-bodied AEC Reliances. Acquisitions included Plaxton-bodied Leopards from Midland Red (three of which had originated with Harper Bros of Heath Hayes) and Ribble, while from Greenslades came AEC Reliances with bodywork by Duple or Plaxton and five Bristol RELH/Plaxtons.

The apparently haphazard application of fleetnames under NBC is demonstrated here by Leyland Leopard PSU5C/Plaxton 256 (DAD 256T). Although it displays 'SOUTH WEST', the slip-board-holder facilitates a quick transfer to another part of the fleet — or, indeed, a holiday contract — when required. No 256 was in its first season when seen leaving Victoria empty, having arrived from Plymouth, in July 1979. *Charles Dean / Author's collection*

Seen when new in April 1977, Leyland Leopard/Plaxton 138 (SDD 138R) heads through the rain at Treharris, Mid Glamorgan, on its way to Cheltenham on route 624 from Treherbert. *John Jones*

In 1977 a number of vehicles were transferred from Greenslades, ahead of the takeover of that company the following year. Among these were 10 AEC Reliances, which arrived in June and worked for just one season. Duple-bodied 176 (NFJ 620G), new in 1969, is seen in Cheltenham on 6 August, unfortunately giving no clue as to the service being operated. *John Jones*

Deliveries in 1976 were split between Leyland Leopard (113-20) and AEC Reliance (150-60), all bodied by Duple. The AECs bore 'SOUTH WEST' fleetnames; having arrived from Llanelli, 154 (NDF 154P) rest at Cheltenham when new. *Author's collection*

From the 1950s to the 1970s it was the practice to delicense part of the fleet during the winter months. Seen stored at Gloucester Docks in December 1976, 142 (AAD 242B), one of the 1964 Plaxton-bodied Leyland Leopards, would complete one more season with Black & White. *Colin Martin*

The premature withdrawal of the Daimler Roadliners necessitated the acquisition of a number of coaches from elsewhere within NBC. Twenty Duple Northern-bodied Leyland Leopards arrived in 1975/6 from Midland Red, including 218 (CHA 118C), seen on its way to Bournemouth in January 1976. The location is Marlborough, outside the erstwhile Good Fare Café, owned by Bristol Omnibus. *Michael Bennett*

The final duty for ex-Southdown Leyland Leopards 193/4 (EUF 191/4D) was as a road-block at the coach station, the usual entrance being sealed off while the road surface was repaired in February 1977. *Colin Martin*

National Travel (West) acquired KCK 918, a Burlingham-bodied Leyland PD3/4 driver trainer, from Ribble in May 1982 and allocated it to Cheltenham, where it was used to instruct Black & White, Wessex and Midland Red drivers. Seen at Cheltenham in January 1983, it went back to Ribble in May 1984. *Colin Martin*

Mention has been made of the small fleet of service vehicles that have been operated. A number of staff cars and vans have been used over the years to enable inspectors to travel around the network and, of course, to collect and deliver such items as publicity material etc. Heavier vehicles included recovery trucks, several of which were owned. One long-serving vehicle was this Atkinson; originally registered 568 CWV as a tractor unit with haulier Bulwark Transport, Chippenham (then part of the Red & White group), it was rebuilt as a tow-truck by Black & White. It ran from 1970 until 1981, being seen here at Cheltenham on trade plate 037 AD in January 1977. *Colin Martin*

The end

By the late 1970s the Black & White identity had become little
more than a fleetname. In March 1978 South West's subsidiary
companies — Wessex National, Greenslades Tours and
Shamrock & Rambler Motor Coaches — all became part of the
main fleet, bringing with them a variety of rolling stock. From
Greenslades came a collection of Leyland Leopoards, AEC
Reliances, Bristol RELHs and LHs and a number of Bedfords,
while Shamrock & Rambler provided a similar mix minus the
Bedfords and LHs; Wessex National's contribution was all-
Bedford with the exception of four Bristol RELHs (ex-Black &
White) and two Leyland Leopards. These acquisitions totalled

93 vehicles, but most did not stay for long, and by the 1980s the
South West fleet had taken on a pretty standardised appearance.
Further restructuring took place in November 1981 with the
takeover of National Travel (South West) operations by National
Travel (West), which itself had been renamed from National
Travel (North West) upon being combined with National Travel
(Midlands) in 1977. By 1981 the operations of National Travel
(South West) were based on just Bristol and Cheltenham, having
passed operations in the West Country at Exeter to Western
National, those at Swansea to South Wales Transport and those
at Southampton and Bournemouth to Hants & Dorset in May
1981. The Black & White fleetname was retained at Cheltenham,
and Wessex at Bristol. Services operated by Black & White

The cramped little coach station at Holdenhurst Road, Bournemouth, plays host to several National coaches in this June 1981 view. Loading for London and bearing 'SOUTH WEST' fleetnames (although these are obscured by a passenger) is 208 (KCK 998H), one of seven Leyland Leopard/ Plaxton coaches acquired from Ribble in 1977. To the right is Black & White 116 (MDF 116P), a 1976 Leyland Leopard/ Duple, Cheltenham-bound on service 770 — a journey of nearly five hours but including a 30min refreshment stop at Salisbury. *Author*

No 112 (PDG 112M), the lone Plaxton-bodied Leyland Leopard delivered new in 1974, is seen on private-hire duty in Boscombe in June 1981. Although ordered by Greenslades, it was delivered to Black & White in exchange for Bristol RELH/Plaxton 330 (ADG 330K). *Author*

under National Travel (West) during this period included:

610/611 (Gloucester/Cheltenham–London)
612 (Cheltenham–Oxford–London)
640 (Cheltenham–Aberystwyth)
647 (Cheltenham–Norwich)
655/657 (Cheltenham–Glasgow/Edinburgh)
741 (Cheltenham–Helston)
770/772 (Cheltenham–Bournemouth)
777 (Cheltenham–Paris)
783 (Cheltenham–Ipswich) and
790 (Cheltenham–Eastbourne)

Operation of the 783 'Eastlander', shared with Premier Travel, Tricentrol and Grey-Green, was particularly unusual: as there was only one return journey each day, each operator would have the service to itself for around six weeks at a time.

As the 1980s progressed, traffic patterns changed as a result of better utilisation of the motorway network, around which it had always been intended that the National Express network should be built, and new interchanges were being developed where motorway access was easier; Birmingham Digbeth and Bristol Marlborough Street were not a million miles from Cheltenham, and the advent of the 70mph coach and the National Express 'Rapide' network all reduced the need to change coaches *en route*. Indeed, a journey from the Midlands to the West Country could comfortably be achieved non-stop with on-board toilets and catering facilities. Cheltenham remained, however, although with a dwindling number of departures daily, and by the 1980s the 14.30 departures had been put back to 15.00. The beginning of the end at Cheltenham was its abolition as an interchange from 22 January 1984 — nearly 50 years since the creation of Associated Motorways. The Summer 1983 National Express timetable listed 598 destinations available from Cheltenham.

Willowbrook bodywork returned to the fleet in 1977 with the delivery of Leyland Leopard PSU3s 124-32 (SAD 124-32R). No 129, by now numbered 429, pauses at The Square, Dunstable, on a Cheltenham-bound 783 in March 1983. The 783 'Eastlander' ran between Ipswich and Cheltenham, but the abolition of Cheltenham as a major interchange brought about its curtailment at Oxford from January 1984 (only to be extended to Bristol and Cardiff, but not via Cheltenham). It remained a joint working, however, between National Travel (West), Premier Travel, Grey-Green and Tricentrol (later Tourmaster) Coaches — operators all now long gone! *Author*

The Cheltenham–Norwich route was plied by Black & White coaches for years. As National Express route 647, in 1983 it entailed just one return journey; Leyland Leopard/Willowbrook 428 (SAD 128R) picks up at Thetford on the 07.50 from Norwich in July that year. Journey time, via Cambridge and Bedford, was 6hr 40min; in 1960 it took about an hour longer. *Author*

Leyland Leopard/Plaxton 302 (SND 302X), new in 1981, stands at Cheltenham on 2 January 1982 prior to departure on National Express route 640 to Milford Haven. *John Jones*

With South West fleetnames, Leyland Leopard/Plaxton 148 (SDD 148R) of 1977 is seen at the premises of Pritchard, Llandrindod Wells, just after Christmas that year. The 640 was the Cheltenham–Aberystwyth service, so presumably this was a duplicate short working or cover for a breakdown. *John Jones*

No 231 (YTX 323H), one of a pair of Leyland Leopard/ Plaxtons acquired from Greenslades Tours in 1974, at Oxford's Gloucester Green bus station in August 1983, by which time the Black & White fleet was under National Travel (West) control. The coach is probably working an Ipswich– Cheltenham journey on service 783, which ran via Luton and Oxford.
Paul Hurst

No 386 (BGY 586T), an AEC Reliance/Plaxton new to National Travel (London), leaves Gloucester for London Victoria in March 1984.
John Jones

Almost the end. Cheltenham lost its interchange status from 22 January 1984; on the 20th, Leyland Leopard PSU5C/Plaxton 346 (KAD 346V) swings out on the penultimate 15.00 790 to Eastbourne, running via Guildford and Brighton. Eastbourne would still be accessible from Cheltenham, however, as part of route 736 (Birmingham–Dover), with a 10.10 departure from Cheltenham. *Stephen Morris*

Wearing stripey National Express livery, Leyland Leopard 429 (SAD 129R) carries Willowbrook 008 Spacecar bodywork — a design launched in 1974 in the face of European imports and also to compete with Plaxton and Duple. In this February 1984 view, 429 leaves Newport on a 609 from Oxford to Cardiff, which ran every two hours via Cheltenham. *Author*

In contrast, the Summer 1984 edition could muster only 50. The much-reduced timetable still saw a few services calling at St Margaret's — the service to London still ran, of course, most journeys starting from Gloucester. There were also two 'Rapides', giving a journey time from Cheltenham to London (Victoria) of 2hr 20min. In 1930 — not a fair comparison, perhaps — it took over five hours!

From 2 June 1984, operations at Cheltenham were transferred within NBC to a separate company — Black & White Motorways Ltd. Fifty-two vehicles changed hands — 38 Leyland Leopards, nine Leyland Tigers, four AEC Reliances and a Leyland Royal Tiger Doyen. Bodywork was from the usual sources — Plaxton, Duple, ECW, Willowbrook and, in the case of the Royal Tiger, Roe. Financial management was provided by local NBC subsidiary Cheltenham & Gloucester Omnibus Co, formed in 1983 upon the division of Bristol Omnibus.

Sadly a revival of old fortunes was not on the cards, and the 'new' Black & White Motorways Ltd operations did not last long, the company being dogged by financial problems and the victim of a declining market. Services operated during this period included the 607 (Gloucester–Cheltenham–London) and 510 'Rapide' (Bristol–London via M4), as well as National Holidays work and the usual private hires etc.

On 28 April 1985 Black & White Motorways was absorbed by Cheltenham & Gloucester, which took on just 17 of the vehicles — a mixture of Leopards, Tigers and the Royal Tiger Doyen, bodied variously by Duple, Plaxton, ECW and Roe — along with around 50 staff. The Black & White title was retained for coaching activities at Cheltenham, such was the respect locally for the old name. Services since the 1985 takeover included the 607 and the 'Rapide' 512 (Gloucester–Cheltenham–London) and the cross-country 773 (Weymouth–Cheltenham–Rugby). The Black & White fleetname was also used for a time on coaches operating from Swindon, including those on limited-stop workings such as the X55 to Chippenham. Several liveries

were used, applied in various stripey styles as was in vogue at the time. Indeed, an early version used dark red and silver stripes along the bodysides, in which scheme the Royal Tiger Doyen looked particularly good.

During the winter of 1985/6 Cheltenham & Gloucester moved all its Cheltenham-based vehicles to St Margaret's and put its own St Mark's depot up for sale. However, no buyer was forthcoming for the latter, so this was refurbished, the buses returned and St Margaret's was declared redundant instead. Thereafter the premises became increasingly derelict and presented a sorry sight to anyone who had known the coach station in its heyday. Demolition came in May 1990, the site later becoming a car park — a role it still fulfils at the time of writing.

Cheltenham & Gloucester was bought from NBC by its management in November 1986. The Black & White image lingered with Cheltenham & Gloucester until the early 1990s, the final livery incorporating black and gold horizontal stripes. Western Travel Ltd, Cheltenham & Gloucester's holding company, was bought by Stagecoach in December 1993, by which time the Black & White image had been allowed to fade away; the handful of coaches transferred — Volvo B10Ms originally with Wallace Arnold — now wore National Express livery. This was not quite the end for the Black & White name, however, as we shall see in the concluding chapter.

 ▲ Of the vehicles in the revived Black & White Motorways fleet, two had interesting histories. The Leyland Leopard chassis of 331/2 (HBP 331/2X) had started life in 1971 with Plaxton Panorama Elite II bodywork as Black & White 329/8 (YDF 329/8K) respectively; by 1981 they were with Shamrock & Rambler, which gave them new Plaxton Supreme IV bodies and new registrations. No 331 is seen on a private-hire working at Llanberis, North Wales, on 1 August 1984 in National Holidays livery, devoid of any Black & White identity. *John Jones*

▲ Black & White 385 (BGY 585T), a Plaxton-bodied AEC Reliance, was one of the vehicles not to pass to Cheltenham & Gloucester on takeover in April 1985. However, along with several others, it was used by C&G while awaiting disposal, which explains its appearance in a pub car park in King's Norton on 29 June! *Tony Neuls*

The last Black & White coach and a return to the Leyland Tiger, albeit a TRCTL11/3RH rather than a TS2! Bodywork was a none-too-common Duple Caribbean 2, seating 50. Numbered 500 and registered B500 TCJ, it stands under the canopy at Cheltenham when new in January 1985. *Colin Martin*

The resurrected Black & White Motorways Ltd lasted less than a year, during which time its fleet was reduced from 52 to 17. Leyland Leopard/Duple 286 (JDG 286V) would not be acquired by Cheltenham & Gloucester, passing instead to National Travel (London), but serves to illustrate the old motif applied to the bootlid. *Colin Martin*

▲ A month or so before the takeover, in March 1985, Leyland Leopard PSU5C/Plaxton 256 (DAD 256T) passes through Victoria at the end of a 607 journey from Gloucester and Cheltenham. *Alec Swain / Author's collection*

▲ In 1985 Cheltenham & Gloucester entered the British Coach Rally with Plaxton Paramount 3500-bodied Leyland Tiger 2215 (B215 WDG), painted in a new 'Black & White' livery incorporating red and silver stripes! The vehicle is seen at Brighton on 21 April 1985 - actually a week before the formal C&G takeover of Black & White Motorways Ltd. *G. R. Mills*

Black & White

1986
MINI BREAK
HOLIDAYS

The final Black & White image with Cheltenham & Gloucester; 2304 (467 WYA), a Leyland Tiger TRCTL11/3R with Plaxton Paramount 3200 bodywork, was new to National Travel (West) in 1983 and served with the short-lived resurrected Black & White Motorways Ltd. Originally registered CDG 206Y, it is seen at Weston-super-Mare in July 1992. *Author's collection*

Another Cheltenham & Gloucester coach to carry the final Black & White livery was Leyland Tiger/Plaxton 2217 (A873 MRW), acquired in 1990 from fellow Western Travel subsidiary Midland Red (South) and seen here on private-hire duty in Southampton. *Author's collection*

Following the temporary closure by Cheltenham & Gloucester Omnibus Co of its St Mark's depot in the town, that company moved its fleet into the coach station, which now saw only a few services. A clutch of Bristol VR and Leyland Olympian double-deckers stand on the forecourt in December 1985. *Colin Martin*

The fleet later moved back to a reopened St Mark's, and the 'For Sale' boards went up at St Margaret's. This was the sorry scene in February 1988. *Colin Martin*

Two years later and the scene was even more sorry, with demolition well underway. The office block has gone, and within a short time the canopy will be down and the site cleared. *Colin Martin*

4. Life after Black & White

In general, Black & White vehicles were well maintained and — with the exception of the Daimler Roadliners — had respectably long lives in the fleet. The prewar Gilfords and Leyland Tigers tended to last between seven and 10 years, while the prewar Bristols were the longest-lived of all Black & White coaches, surviving for between 17 and 19 years; the 1948/9 L6Gs were all sold after 12 years of service. The various underfloor-engined types fared about the same, generally seeing between 11 and 14 years' service. The Daimlers rather let the side down, the four batches delivered during the years 1967-70 being withdrawn after four, five, six and five years respectively. The longest-lived Roadliner, re-engined, managed nine years' service, no less (although how long it spent under repair is probably another story!).

Most Black & White vehicles found new owners, after passing initially to dealers such as North's and Frank Cowley. The Bristols were generally too old to see further service, but the relatively youthful Daimlers all found new owners willing to coax a bit more life out of them.

A few Black & White vehicles have survived into preservation. The oldest to survive is 1929 Leyland TS2 DF 8420, formerly L37. Withdrawn after the war, it was one of those that had been converted to ARP ambulances in 1939; by 1947 it was with Jennings, Bude, who had it fitted with a new Duple body in 1949. It passed to the West of England Transport Collection in March 1962, but has since moved on. Bristol L6G/Duple HDD 654 is with Black & White (formerly Classic Buses), Winchester, as are Guy Arabs NDG 172 and SAD 189, Leopards 6775/9 DD and Roadliner RDG 304G. Other Black & White vehicles known to be still in existence include Leopard HDG 268D and Roadliners KDD 276E, RDG 308G and UAD 316H. It would, however, be misleading to imply that the spirit of Black & White survives only in its vehicles, for the annual staff reunion still draws up to a hundred former employees and enthusiasts.

The 1929 Leyland-bodied Leyland TS2s were disposed of between 1937 and 1945. Nos L27, 35-7/9 were converted for use as ARP ambulances in 1939, which explains their survival through much of the war, but L32 (DF 8186) was withdrawn in 1938, passing (via a dealer) to Green, London W6, who appears to have traded as Empress. By now numbered 14, it is seen after the war at Worthing, still looking smart. It was sold for scrap in 1953. *Author's collection*

A number of Black & White vehicles ended up with Gloucestershire independent Edwards, Lydbrook, including three of the 1964 Harrington-bodied AEC Reliances. One of these was the former A250 (AAD 250B), seen leaving the Rank Xerox factory at Mitcheldean on contract duties in September 1981. A former Southdown Marshall-bodied Leyland Leopard, also with Edwards, is in pursuit. *John Jones*

A number of coaches passed from National Travel (South West) to subsidiary Greenslades Tours in 1976, including the 10 Leyland Leopard PSU3s delivered in 1965. Harrington-bodied former L256/3 (DDG 256/3C) are pictured in store at Staverton Airport in July of that year. *John Jones*

▲ Daimler Roadliner SRP8 D316 (UAD 316H) of 1970 has now
passed into preservation, although at one time, following
withdrawal by Staffordshire independent Knotty Bus & Coach
Co in 1995, its chances of survival appeared slim. Previously,
in 1989, it made an appearance at Showbus, Woburn, in an early
'preserved' state. *Author's collection*

Withdrawn in 1954, Bristol JO6G B79 (BAD 632) ended its days in Ireland. Having worked for Killiney Castle Coaches and Dunne, Maryborough, by the early 1960s it had been put out to grass in a Portlaoise scrapyard. Carrying its 1941 Duple body, it was photographed in July 1969. *Peter Tulloch*

Another Irish exile was L137 (KDF 988), from the 1951 batch of Leyland Royal Tigers with Willowbrook bodies. By August 1965 it was with Glynn, Graigue-na-Spidogue, and a year later appeared still to be in Black & White livery. *Peter Tulloch*

The 1948 batch of 10 Duple-bodied Bristol L6G coaches were withdrawn in 1960, all passing initially to dealer Alexander & Tatham. Six were bought by T. D. Alexander, who operated from Sheffield and Arbroath. The former B110 and B113 (HDD 653/6) and another appeared to be engaged on contract work when photographed *c*1962 in the Doncaster area. *Author's collection*

Bristol L6G/Duple B111 (HDD 654) had a happier history; sold by Alexander & Tatham to South Wales operator Chapple, Raglan, it survived long enough to be bought for preservation in 1970. *Peter Tulloch*

▲ A pair of Guy Arab LUFs were rescued for preservation in 1998,
Willowbrook-bodied former G189 (SAD 189) and Duple-bodied G172
(NDG 172) having resided in a sandpit for the previous 20 years; they
had been amongst several Black & White vehicles to have passed to
Birmingham contractor Douglas. G189 is seen shortly after removal for
restoration at the premises of the reborn Black & White Motorways Ltd,
as mentioned opposite, in May 1998. *Gerry Serpell-Morris*

▲ The name of Black & White Motorways lives on at what was formerly
Classic Buses, Winchester. Having discovered that the name was no longer
registered, proprietor Peter Bailey took steps to acquire it, and his fleet,
used mainly on private hires and contracts, was repainted into traditional
Black & White livery, including a double-decker, former Southampton
Leyland Atlantean 195. Several genuine Black & White vehicles are owned,
including the two Guy Arabs and Plaxton bodied Leyland Leopard L225
(6775 DD), withdrawn back in 1973 and seen here in the company
of AEC Reliance/Plaxton XYE 101G. *Philip Lamb*

▲ Despite their unreliability, the youthful Daimler Roadliners managed
to find new homes. No D308 (RDG 308G), a 1969 SRP8, had passed
through three other operators before reaching Carr of Charing Heath,
Kent, in 1983 and still looked the part after 14 years.
Author's collection

Despite appearances, this is a Black & White disposal. Upon the Cheltenham & Gloucester takeover, 10 vehicles passed to National Travel (London), of which at least one carried a combination of 'BLACK & WHITE' and 'NATIONAL LONDON' fleetnames! Still in full B&W livery, Leyland Leopard PSU5C/Duple JDG 286V arrives at Victoria from Clacton and Walton-on-the-Naze in May 1985. *Alec Swain / Author's collection*

When is Black & White not Black & White? I suspect that this vehicle has confused a few enthusiasts in its time. New in 1979 as National Travel (South West) 280 (GDF 280V), this Leyland Leopard PSU5/Duple passed to Hants & Dorset in 1981 and thence to Hampshire Bus. By May 1987 it was with Black & White Coaches, Scunthorpe, with which operator it is seen at London Victoria a year later on National Express duties. *Author*

A gathering of preserved coaches took place at the site of Cheltenham coach station on 1 July 2001, marking 70 years since its opening. Gerry Serpell-Morris attended with his well-known Black & White-liveried VW caravanette with part of his collection of memorabilia, including a model of the coach station itself, now at the Oxford Bus Museum. They are seen displayed on the chequered black and white floor tiles formerly under the café and still surviving as part of the car park. *Gerry Serpell-Morris*

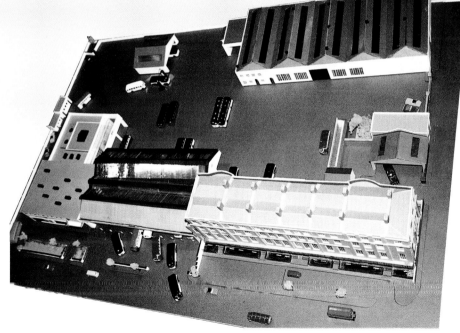

A selection of memorabilia from Gerry Serpell-Morris's collection; the Associated Motorways flag formerly flew over the coach station.

Bibliography

The following publications have been helpful in the compilation this volume:

Black & White — A Pictorial Reminiscence, 1926-1976, published by the Oxford Bus Preservation Syndicate, 1976;

PSV Circle Fleet History PH4;

Various periodicals and newspapers including:

Bus & Coach
Bus & Coach Preservation
Buses
Buses Extra
Classic Bus
Coaching Journal
Motor Transport
The Omnibus Magazine
The Gloucestershire Echo

Also numerous timetables and other publicity from Black & White Motorways, Associated Motorways and National Travel.

One website has been of particular use — the excellent www.blackandwhitemotorways.co.uk

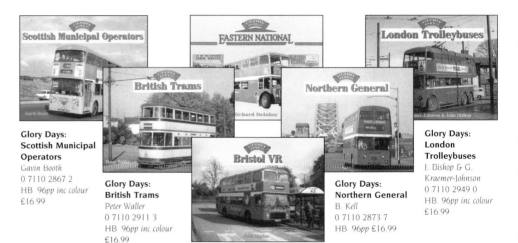